# FACT AND FICTION
## IN
## B. F. SKINNER'S SCIENCE & UTOPIA
(An Essay on Philosophy of Psychology)

# FACT AND FICTION

## IN

# B. F. SKINNER'S SCIENCE & UTOPIA

### (An Essay on Philosophy of Psychology)

*By*

**R. PULIGANDLA**

*Department of Philosophy*
*University of Toledo*
*Toledo, Ohio*

**WARREN H. GREEN, INC.**
*St. Louis, Missouri, U.S.A.*

*Published by*

WARREN H. GREEN, INC.
10 South Brentwood Boulevard
Saint Louis, Missouri 63105, U.S.A.

*Library of Congress Catalog Card Number 73-21001*
*ISBN NO. 0-87527-130-8*

*Printed in the United States of America*

*To*
Professor Herbert Feigl
*in*
*appreciation of his learning and friendship*

## About the Author

Born in India in 1930, Ramakrishna Puligandla was educated in his native country and the U.S. He holds graduate degrees in Engineering and Physics and received the Ph.D. degree in Philosophy in 1966 from Rice University. His areas of specialty are Philosophy of Science and Comparative Philosophy. He has published a number of articles in scholarly and professional journals. His forthcoming books include *The Copenhagen Interpretation of Quantum Theory* and *Indian Philosophy*, to be published by Motilal Banarsidass, India and Abingdon Press, U.S., respectively. He is currently Professor of Philosophy at the University of Toledo (Ohio).

# ACKNOWLEDGMENTS

The author wishes to thank the graduate students in his epistemology and philosophy of science seminars who, through their searching questions, have forced him to do careful thinking on some of the issues discussed in this book. He is especially thankful to Mrs. Kay Wenzel for her meticulous and elegant typing of the manuscript and other secretarial assistance.

# PREFACE

The purpose of this essay is to critically examine B. F. Skinner's science of behavior and behavioral utopia, with special reference to his *Beyond Freedom and Dignity.* * Special attention will be paid to Skinner's claim that his utopia is based on scientific analysis (a term he is extremely fond of) of human behavior, individually as well as collectively. It will be shown that, contrary to Skinner's repeated assertions, there is hardly anything scientific about his purported arguments and analyses. For one thing, most of his observations on human behavior are nothing but common sense and folk wisdom dressed up in pseudo-scientific jargon and supported by strawman arguments. Further, at crucial points, his arguments either beg the questions at issue or avoid them altogether through the well-known devices of trite phrases and impersonal ad hominems.

I have made it a point to avoid attacking Skinner on nonintellectual grounds, which are the source of much indignation, wrath, and contempt unleashed on him in reviews, talk-shows, and letters to editors. Shocking as it may seem to many, I have not concerned myself in the present book with whether Skinner's design of culture is good, bad, or dangerous and whether it should be condemned or commended. Such questions are irrelevant to an examination of Skinner's analyses of science, man, freedom, culture, and control from a purely intellectual point of view and it is as intellectual issues I am going to deal with them here.

One final point: showing that Skinner's analyses are mistaken and his theses unproven and unwarranted does not constitute a defense and proof of their contraries or contradictories. One would be missing the whole point about the nature of Skinner's claims were one to think so. In short, Skinner's theses are metaphysical theses and in matters metaphysical, no

---

*B. F. Skinner, *Beyond Freedom and Dignity,* Alfred Knopf, Inc., N.Y., 1971.

matter how thickly camouflaged, there can be no question of truth or falsehood—only whether one is persuaded to accept them or not. It is true, however, that metaphysical theses serve as directives for constructing scientific theories whose consequences can be put to experimental test.** But insofar as Skinner rejects theorizing as unworthy of his science, all he has are pure metaphysical assertions on the one hand and observations crying for explanations on the other. The present study is a demonstration that Skinner's central theses are dogmatic metaphysics, prejudice, and bias presented in the guise of science.

---

**See Stephen Körner, *Conceptual Thinking,* Dover Publications, Inc., N.Y., 1959, especially chapters xxx-xxxiii.

R. Puligandla and K. Puhakka, "Körner's Theory of Scientific and Metaphysical Directives." *The Journal of the Indian Academy of Philosophy,* Calcutta, 1970, Vol. ix, No. 1, pp. 34-49.

# CONTENTS

FACT AND FICTION
IN
B. F. SKINNER'S SCIENCE & UTOPIA
(An Essay on Philosophy of Psychology)

# *Chapter I*

## INTRODUCTION

It is well-known that there are many schools of psychology, of which the behaviorist, the gestalt, and the Freudian are the most prominent. The first two are generally regarded as basic sciences which study the behavior of organisms in their various psychological aspects, whereas the third is thought of primarily as applied psychology whose aim is to understand and cure mental illness in its diverse manifestations. Gestalt psychology is widely practised on the Continent, while behaviorism reigns supreme in Great Britain and the United States. J. B. Watson (1878-1958) is generally regarded as the founder of modern behaviorism as a method of psychological inquiry and B. F. Skinner is credited with having perfected it and demonstrated its power and fecundity in the study of the behavior of organisms, including man. Appropriately enough, Skinner and his followers describe themselves as radical behaviorists. What is radical behaviorism? In order to answer this question, let us first briefly describe behaviorism.

Behaviorism arose as a reaction against the traditional conception of man as made up of two radically different kinds of entities, namely, body and mind. This view of man, although at least as old as Plato, was clearly formulated by the French philosopher and mathematician, René Descartes (1596-1650). According to Descartes, man is a combination of two substances, the mental and the physical, thought being the attribute of the former and extension that of the latter. Once such a fundamental dichotomy had been announced, men began to wonder how two such totally disparate entities as mind and body interacted. Descartes himself maintained that the interaction

1

took place in the pineal gland, and other philosophers proposed their own solutions to this riddle which has since been referred to as the "mind-body problem." Monism, dualism, parallelism, occasionalism, and prestablished harmony are various attempts to explain how mind and body act upon each other. It became increasingly mysterious as to how my willing to raise my hand results in the raising of my hand. It seemed to many that man is the meeting point of two orders of reality, will, desire, purpose, intention, etc. belonging to the mental order and his bodily movements to the physical order.

Those philosophers and psychologists who try to explain the observed behavior of man through concepts and categories of the mental order and who maintain that these cannot be reduced to those of the physical order are known as 'mentalists.' On the other hand, those who hold that mentalistic concepts and categories provide only unscientific, pseudo-explanations of observed behavior and that only explanations employing concepts and categories whose meanings can be exhaustively set forth in terms of publicly observable and performable operations have come to be known as 'physicalists.' Behaviorism is a particular variety of physicalism in that it maintains that all behavior is to be accounted for only through what is observable. The distinction between mild and wild behaviorisms depends upon the nature and extent of concessions one allows to the role of mentalistic as well as theoretical concepts (concepts not wholly definable through observational vocabulary) in the study of behavior. We may now characterize radical behaviorism as that school of psychology which attempts to study behavior purely in terms of the publicly observable and verifiable, and eschews all mentalistic and theoretical concepts, such as 'introspection,' 'consciousness,' 'mind,' 'purpose,' 'intention,' 'libido,' etc.—in short, anything that is supposedly accessible only to the subject and goes under his skin and hence not open to objective inspection and analysis.

According to the program of radical behaviorism, then, all descriptions and explanations of behavior which employ mentalistic and subjective categories are to be rejected as unscientific, unverifiable, and metaphysical. Closely akin to radical behaviorism are operationalism and logical positivism, according to which the meaning of every concept that can figure in scientific descriptions and explanations of phenomena should be exhaustively specifiable through operations that are in principle publicly performable and observable. Some operationalists have gone so far as to claim that a concept is nothing more than a set of operations and *the concept is synonymous with the corresponding set of operations.*[1] Any concept that cannot be, so to speak, operationalized, is to be rejected as meaningless. According to the positivists, all meaningful statements fall into one or the other of two classes: the analytic and the empirical.[2] The meaning and truth of the former kind of statements can be determined solely on the basis of the meanings of their constitutive terms and the syntactical rules of the language (including rules of logic) in which the statements are expressed—that is, no inspection of the world is needed for determining the truth or falsity of such statements. On the other hand, the second kind of statements depend for their truth on the world around us. Thus '2 + 2 = 4,' "bachelors are unmarried males," and "everything that is red is colored" are analytic statements; and "copper conducts electricity," "Nixon is the present President of the U.S.," "kangaroos abound in Australia," and "the mass of the electron is $9.1 \times 10^{-31}$ kg" are empirical statements. Any statement that is neither analytic nor empirical is to be regarded as meaningless and nonsensical. Thus ethical, theological, religious, and metaphysical statements are relegated to the category of nonsensical statements. Radical behaviorism is thus an ally of and in an important sense indistinguishable from operationalism and logical positivism. There is no need here to present detailed criticisms of such a narrowly conceived empiricism. The most severe and devastating criticisms of it we owe to W. V. O. Quine and P. K. Feyerabend.[3]

---

[1] P. W. Bridgman, *The Logic of Modern Physics,* Macmillan, N.Y., 1927, p. 5.

[2] A. J. Ayer, *Language, Truth, and Logic,* Dover Publications, Inc., N.Y., 1946.

[3] Paul K. Feyerabend, "How to be a Good Empiricist—A Plea for Tolerance in Matters Epistemological," *Philosophy of Science, The Delaware Seminar,* Vol. 2, ed. B. Baumrin, Interscience Publishers, N.Y., 1963, pp. 3-39.

Paul K. Feyerabend, "Explanation, Reduction, and Empiricism," *Minnesota Studies in the Philosophy of Science,* Vol. III, University of Minnesota Press, Minneapolis, 1962, pp. 28-97.

W. V. O. Quine, "Two Dogmas of Empiricism," *From a Logical Point of View,* Harper & Row, N.Y., 1963, pp. 20-46.

Central to the behavioristic program is the concept of conditioning. Drawing inspiration from the Russian physiologist Ivan Pavlov's (1849-1936) concept of conditioned reflex and developing that of operant conditioning, behaviorism asserts that all behavior, including verbal behavior, can be described and explained through what has come to be known as the stimulus-response paradigm, briefly the S-R paradigm. According to this paradigm, all behavior is response emitted by an organism to some stimulus or other in its environment. To be sure, it is not at all clear as to how to precisely define 'stimulus,' 'response,' and 'environment.' Various definitions have been proposed and none of them commands unaminous acceptance.[4]

Another important concept of behaviorism is 'reinforcement.'

> A much more important role is played by behavior which weakens harmful stimuli in another way. It is not acquired in the form of conditioned reflexes, but as the product of a different process called operant conditioning. When a bit of behavior is followed by a certain kind of consequence, it is more likely to occur again, and a consequence having this effect is called a reinforcer. Food, for example, is a reinforcer to a hungry organism; anything the organism does that is followed by receipt of food is more likely to be done again whenever the organism is hungry. Some stimuli are called negative reinforcers; any response which reduces the intensity of such a stimulus—or ends it—is more likely to be emitted when the stimulus recurs. Thus, if a person escapes from a hot sun when he moves under cover, he is more likely to move under cover when the sun is again hot. The reduction in temperature reinforces the behavior it is "contingent upon"—that is, the behavior it follows. Operant conditioning also occurs when a person simply avoids a hot sun—when roughly speaking, he escapes from the *threat* of the hot sun.[5]

It is clear that for Skinner's behaviorism operant conditioning is the key technique by which to modify and control the behavior of organisms.

---

[4]Merle B. Turner, *Philosophy and the Science of Behavior*, Appleton-Century-Crofts, N.Y., 1967, pp. 198-202.

[5]B. F. Skinner, *Beyond Freedom and Dignity* (hereafter abbreviated as "B. F. D."), Alfred Knopf, Inc., N.Y., 1971, p. 27.

Crucial to all discussions of scientific method is the role of theoretical terms in scientific theory and practice. In this context, it is a general practice to divide terms into two types: observational and theoretical, although it is not always easy to draw a sharp line of demarcation between them. Thus 'volume,' 'red,' 'floats,' 'wood,' 'cell nucleus' are examples of observational terms in the sense that their meanings can be explicitly and exhaustively stated in terms of observation. On the other hand, terms such as 'aggressive,' 'drive,' 'motive,' 'intention,' 'libido,' 'id,' 'ego,' 'hungry,' 'temperature,' 'soluble,' 'electron,' 'gravitational field,' 'gene,' 'virus,' etc. are theoretical terms whose meanings, unlike those of observational terms, cannot be exhaustively specified through observations and observable operations. Physicists, biologists, and psychologists all employ theoretical terms. But the question is how they are to be understood and their role interpreted. Once again, there is no unanimous agreement among scientists and philosophers on these issues. Thus at the one extreme we have those who freely admit and retain theoretical terms as essential to science and at the other those who maintain that either the so-called theoretical terms, if used at all, are completely translatable into observational terms or that the former are not needed at all for science. Skinner and other radical behaviorists not only claim to reject all theoretical terms and theorizing as unnecessary for a science of behavior but also consider them as positive hindrance to it. There has accumulated a large body of writings on the controversy surrounding the nature, status, and role of theoretical terms.[6] We need not go here into these writings. Suffice it to mention that radical behaviorists believe that to admit theoretical terms, insofar as they resist total translation into observational vocabulary, is to not only swerve from the austere path of a wholly empirical science but also surreptitiously acknowledge the ex-

---

[6]For an excellent and incisive treatment of theoretical terms, see Carl G. Hempel, "The Theoretician's Dilemma: A Study in the Logic of Theory Construction," *Aspects of Scientific Explanation,* The Free Press, N.Y., 1965, pp. 173-226.

Also Grover Maxwell, "The Ontological Status of Theoretical Entities," *Minnesota Studies in the Philosophy of Science,* Vol. III, ed. H. Feigl and G. Maxwell, University of Minnesota Press, Minneapolis, 1962.

Peter Achinstein, "The Problem of Theoretical Terms," *American Philosophical Quarterly,* II, No. 3, July, 1965.

istence of some invisible, intangible, and ghostly entities, properties, states, and processes which are neither needed nor should
be appealed to in a truly scientific study of behavior. Needless
to say, what goes on inside the organism and what is not
observable in its overt behavior are, according to radical behaviorists, the staple diet of the mentalist and the mystery-monger
and hence have no place in a science of behavior. It will be
shown, however, in the chapters to follow, that the behaviorist
can neither get rid of theoretical terms nor translate them into
wholly observational terms and that there can be no such thing
as theory-neutral observational language. Observation cannot
take place in a vacuum and it is futile to pretend that it does.
Even such a fundamental act as classification, as distinguished
from naming, presupposes a theoretical background of properties, processes, and relations not all of which can be located in
the observable.[7] The radical behaviorist cannot make good his
claim to reject all theoretical terms and theorizing.

Let us now consider the main features of science. It is
generally recognized that the three goals of science are description, explanation, and prediction of phenomena. The radical
behaviorist, too, acknowledges these as the proper aim of
science. But, unfortunately for it, radical behaviorism, insofar as
it refuses to go beyond the publicly observable behavior, can at
best provide only description of behavior but cannot explain and
predict it in a nontrivial sense. This is particularly true of
Skinner's science of behavior in that he firmly maintains that he
need not concern himself with the findings of behavioral
biology, physiology, and neuropsychology, the disciplines which
study the physico-chemical mechanisms of organisms in terms of
which to account for from a fundamental level the observed
behavior of organisms. By rejecting these disciplines as unnecessary for his study of behavior, Skinner's supposed explanations
and predictions are either common sense observations or downright tautologies (a tautology is a non-informative, repetitive
statement which is true under all circumstances, actual or
possible). That this is indeed the case with respect to Skinner's

---

[7]Hugh G. Petrie, "A Dogma of Operationalism in the Social Sciences,"
*Philosophy of the Social Sciences,* Vol. I, 1971, pp. 145-160.

explanations of behavior, if there are any, will be shown in detail later. No wonder, despite all his claims that his science of behavior follows the path of physics and biology, Skinner's behaviorism still remains and will remain an inefficient and limited technology of behavior but not a science which can explain and predict behavior. Skinner's single-minded refusal to consider behavior from levels other than that of overt behavior (the molar level) is the main source of its inability to explain and predict behavior.

In saying all this, I do not wish to convey the impression that the whole work of Skinner and his followers is useless, unimportant, and insignificant. The detailed experimental work, spanning over three decades, in operant conditioning and reinforcement schedules, for which Skinner is justly famous, is surely a necessary step toward a science of behavior. But in itself such work is incapable of explaining and predicting behavior. The S-R correlations gathered by painstaking laboratory work serve as the raw data at the phenomenological level from which to start explanation and prediction of beahvior by relating the data to the findings of neurophysiology and behavioral biology. Unless and until the findings of behaviorism are related to these fundamental sciences, all we have are descriptions of molar behavior and a limited ability to control it. Skinner's behaviorism stands to behavioral biology as phenomenological thermodynamics does to statistical mechanics. Thus it is appropriate to describe radical behaviorism more as a technology than as a science of behavior. And a science which can only provide descriptions of behavior at the overt level but which lacks the ability to explain and predict it is at best a pseudo-science. I turn now to a detailed examination of Skinner's theses and claims.

# Chapter II

## SKINNER'S CONCEPTION OF SCIENCE

In this chapter, I shall set forth and examine certain of Skinner's views and claims concerning science in general and that of behavior in particular. These deal with a variety of issues ranging from scientific method to the possibility of a science of behavior. On each issue I shall first quote Skinner and then examine what he says.

Commenting on the advanced stage and secure status of physics and biology and bemoaning a lack of similar success on the part of psychology, Skinner writes:

> Physics and biology moved farther away from personified causes when they began to attribute the behavior of things to essences, qualities, or natures.[8]

But, he continues,

> almost everyone who is concerned with human affairs—as political scientist, philosopher, man of letters, economist, psychologist, linguist, sociologist, theologian, anthropologist, educator, or psychotherapist—continues to talk about human behavior in this pre-scientific way. Every issue of a daily paper, every magazine, every professional journal, every book with any bearing whatsoever on human behavior will supply examples. We are told that to control the number of people in the world we need to change *attitudes* toward children, overcome *pride* in size of family or in sexual potency, build some *sense of responsibility* toward offspring, and reduce the role played by a large family in allaying *concern* for old age.... To allay the disaffection of the young we must provide a *sense of purpose,* and reduce feelings of *alienation* or *hopelessness.* ... This is staple fare. Almost no one questions it. Yet there is nothing like it in modern physics or most of biology, and that fact may

---

[8]B. F. Skinner, *B. F. D.,* p. 9.

well explain why a science and a technology of behavior have been so long delayed.[9]

He then goes on to say that the primary obstacle to a science of behavior is a

> longstanding conviction that for much of human behavior there *are* no relevant antecedents. The function of the inner man is to provide an explanation which will not be explained in turn. Explanation stops with him. He is not a mediator between past history and current behavior, he is a *center* from which behavior emanates. He initiates, originates, and creates, and in doing so he remains, as he was for the Greeks, divine. We say that he is autonomous—and, so far as a science of behavior is concerned, that means miraculous.[10]

It is certainly true that physics and, to a lesser extent, biology have quite sometime ago emancipated themselves from essences, natures, occult forces, personified causes, and purposes as explanatory concepts. But have they also given up theories and hypotheses and turned directly to the relation between a phenomenon and its environment ignoring and neglecting mediating concepts, entities, and states? Skinner commends Newton for the latter's famous dictum "Hypotheses non-fingo" but laments that Newton was not quite as good as his word.[11] I wish to point out that it is fortunate for us that Newton did not take his own dictum literally and seriously, for otherwise he could not have erected the great structure known as classical physics. Contrary to Skinner's mistaken belief, Newton's physics is full of hypotheses, theoretical concepts, hypothetical entities, and mediating states, such as 'gravitational field,' 'action-at-a-distance,' 'inertia,' 'corpuscles of light,' etc. None of these is given in direct observation of falling bodies, planetary motion, tides, and optical phenomena. Post-Newtonian physics, too, contains theoretical concepts, such as 'atoms,' 'thermodynamical increase in entropy,' 'aether,' 'electromagnetic field,' 'the quantum of action,' 'absolute velocity of light,' 'Schrödinger's quantum mechanical wave' (represented by the psi-function), none of which is given in direct observation. But

---

[9]B. F. Skinner, *B. F. D.*, pp. 9-10.
[10]*Ibid.*, p. 14.
[11]*Ibid.*, p. 9.

the *fact* of such concepts needs stressing, because they are seldom recognized, even by philosophers of science outside the ranks of physics. Their enormous power in scientific explanation need hardly be mentioned (though occasionally one may be discredited, like the aether). *It has never proved possible to dispense with them*; nor is this necessary; for, despite the unobservability of what they designate, *such concepts are used in hypotheses that are tested by observation.* In short, the widely overlooked message is that mysterious entities can be used in the hypothetico-deductive framework culminating in empirical/observational test.

*There is no reason to rule out a priori the possibility of proceeding along the same lines* in the social sciences. Success through their use is not guaranteed, but it is reasonable to try them.[12]

Physics thrives on theoretical concepts and were it not for them, physics would still be a pseudo-science like Skinner's behaviorism. Thus it is simply false to say that physics has become a full-fledged science by turning its attention to solely what is directly observable. Let me explain this point by an illustration. Robert Boyle discovered, on the basis of empirical study of gases, the well-known Boyle's law—temperature remaining constant, the pressure of a given mass of gas varies inversely as its volume. This is a true empirical law. But how does one *explain* it? Not by further confirming it by studying the behavior of some more gases. Boyle's law is merely a true empirical generalization of the behavior of gases at the phenomenological level and no explanation of it can come from that level. One has to move to some other level which necessarily involves concepts and entities not present at the phenomenological level. This is precisely what had been done when Boyle's law had been deduced from the kinetic theory of gases, which postulates molecules, point-masses, mean-free paths, perfectly elastic collisions, etc. All these serve to explain the empirically observed behavior of gases as expressed by Boyle's law.

It would be interesting to ask Skinner how the relation between behavior and environment are given in the absence of any theoretical background whatsoever. It is notoriously clear that a given behavior can be analyzed in more than one way on

---

[12]J. O. Wisdom, "Science versus the Scientific Revolution," *Philosophy of the Social Sciences,* Vol. I, 1971, pp. 135 (emphasis added).

the basis of different criteria of observation and description. More importantly, the notion of a theory-neutral language as well as that of a purely factual language is a fond myth:

> Consider the factual language of behaviorism itself. From Watson on, behaviorists have concurred that the basic data of psychology are to be behavior itself. That the basic facts of psychology are to be publicly observed responses was taken so much for granted that few writers were to give more than passing attention to the concept of response itself. Strangely, however, psychologists who could reach significant methodological agreements differed as to the language of fact. Behaviorists generally have agreed that the response language is a molar rather than molecular language; it speaks of complex coordinations and movements of the organism rather than of reflexes and muscle twitches. *Yet the terminology adopted by the theoretical behaviorists shows such diversity that we know it is impossible to separate language of fact from that of theory....* Class membership depends on definitions wherein the conceptual framework is all-important... *a fact is a general proposition determined by the conceptual predispositions of the factual classifier....* The raw data are neutral, so to speak, but they are unexpressed. *Facts cannot be neutral for they reflect our classificatory penchants....* Why, we should then ask, just this set of defining properties for the factual class and not another? What determines the relevant items of response from the irrelevant? What determines the defining properties of behavior? Doubtless, *the answer is to be found in the conceptual framework which the behaviorist brings to his study of learning (behavior).*[13]

Skinner uses the term 'susceptibility' in "A susceptibility to negative reinforcement is equally important."[14] 'Susceptibility,' like 'solubility' is a dispositional term. But the question is how to explicate it on wholly behavioral criteria. Skinner also uses the terms 'aggressive' and 'intention.'[15] All these are theoretical terms, which may be divided into dispositional and non-dispositional terms. Terms like 'aggressive,' 'hungry,' 'soluble,' and 'magnetic' are dispositional and those like 'intention,' 'motive,' 'electron' are non-dispositional. The reason why 'soluble' is

---

[13]Merle B. Turner, *Philosophy and the Science of Behavior*, Appleton-Century-Crofts, N.Y., 1967, pp. 190-194 (emphasis added).

[14]Skinner, *B. F. D.*, p. 104.

[15]*Ibid.*, p. 108.

regarded as a dispositional term is that when we say x is soluble
we mean that when x is put into a solvent x will dissolve, not
necessarily that x is dissolving at the time the statement is made.
Similarly, when we say x is aggressive we mean that x has a
disposition to behave in certain ways under certain circumstances, not necessarily that he is behaving so when the statement is made. Terms such as 'motive,' 'intention,' 'drive,' and
'electron' are non-dispositional theoretical terms because they
can be thought of as referring not to dispositions and tendencies
but to some hypothetical entities, states, and processes which
are not directly observable and yet are necessary for explanation
and prediction. We shall now point out the difficulties associated
with defining theoretical terms, whether dispositional or non-
dispositional, through wholly behavioral (observational, operational) terms.

Let us denote "x is aggressive" by "AX," "x is under
contingencies C" by "Cx," and "x displays behavior B" by
"Bx." Then a behavioral definition of "x is aggressive" is written
as:

$$Ax \leftrightarrow (Cx \rightarrow Bx) \qquad (1)$$

where the logical connectives "↔" and "→" stand for "if and
only if" and "if . . . then," respectively. (1) is read as "x is
aggressive if and only if (if x is under contingencies C, then x
displays behavior B)." But the trouble with this definition is that
we will be compelled to say that x is aggressive even when he is
not under contingencies C. Thus the mildest man should be
regarded as aggressive as long as he is not under contingencies C.
This predicament arises out of the logical character of "→" and
"↔," because "Cx → Bx" is false just in case "Cx" is true and
"Bx" is false; it is true otherwise; and "Ax ↔ (Cx → Bx)" is true
just in case both "Ax" and "(Cx → Bx)" are true or false; it is
false otherwise. Thus assume "Cx" is false, that is, x is not
under contingencies C. Then no matter what "Bx" is, true or
false, "(Cx → Bx)" will be true, and this in turn means "Ax ↔
(Cx → Bx)" is true. Thus one has to say that x is aggressive even
when x is not under contingencies C. It is not possible to
circumvent this difficulty and still have an exclusively operational (behavioral) definition of terms like 'aggressive,' 'hungry,'

'motive,' 'drive,' 'intention,' 'electron,' 'gene,' etc. The philosopher Rudolf Carnap, having noticed this difficulty, proposed a modification of the operational definition resulting in what are known as "Carnap's reduction sentences." The reduction sentence corresponding to (1) is: $Cx \rightarrow (Ax \leftrightarrow Bx)$, read as "If x is under contingencies C, then (x is aggressive if and only if x displays behavior B). This formulation has the virtue of not compelling us to say whether or not x is aggressive when he is not under contingencies C. But such a virtue is bought at the price of giving up an exhaustively behavioral definition of 'aggressive.' That is, the reduction sentence provides only a partial explication of theoretical terms. These limitations apply equally to all theoretical terms, whether dispositional or non-dispositional. All this is familiar to students of philosophy of science. The point of these observations, then, is that Skinner's claim that his science of behavior is solely based on observable behavior is untenable and false, insofar as dispositional terms are central to his science, as he himself admits. I am not hereby, however, suggesting that appeals be made to the autonomous man in order to explain human behavior. All I am saying is that a science solely based on the observable is a myth.

One does not have to accept Aristotle's physics and biology in order to recognize his insight into the nature of explanation. According to Aristotle, no body of knowledge can claim to be scientific unless it has a theory, a theory being that which enables one to link one fact with another, or one phenomenon with another. Aristotle was fully aware that a given number of facts (Skinner's purely "observational statements"), no matter how large, cannot explain a phenomenon. It is only by inventing and forging theoretical concepts (concepts which cannot be exhaustively defined through observational data) can one glue facts into a network and explain and account for what is observed. That Aristotle's theoretical concepts, such as 'purpose' and 'entelechy,' did not lead to fruitful explanation and prediction of even such a simple fact that bodies fall to the ground with increasing speeds does not mean that we should reject not only Aristotle's particular explanations but also his concept of explanation as necessarily involving theoretical concepts and entities. People have been observing for a long time that bodies fall to the ground with increasing speeds. But why did they not come up with an explanation of this phenomenon? Why did the world have to wait until Galileo and Newton? Underlying Newton's explanation of freely falling bodies is the concept of gravitational attraction. But no one observes gravitational attraction as one does freely-falling bodies. 'Gravitational attraction' is a theoretical concept by means of which to explain the phenomenon of freely falling bodies.

It is interesting that in a certain sense Aristotle and Skinner are much closer to each other than Skinner himself believes when he writes "no modern physicist or biologist would turn to Aristotle for help."[16] Both are thoroughgoing empiricists and for that reason both produced barren science. Sticking close to what is observed, Aristotle could not formulate the concept of inertia and the result is a physics which only provided pseudo-explanations and no predictions at all. Skinner, too, refusing to go beyond overt behavior and rejecting theoretical concepts, produced a psychology which is totally incapable of explaining and predicting behavior, although capable of a limited control of behavior. That Aristotle was too much of an empiricist is clear from his treatment of motion.[17] Thus, having observed that a ball rolled on the ground eventually comes to rest, he thought of force as that which is needed to keep the ball in a state of constant motion. Compare this with the Newtonian concept of force as that which changes or tends to change the state of rest or of uniform motion of a body in a straight line. To be sure, Newton did not observe anything different from what Aristotle did with respect to a ball rolled on the ground. Where, then, is the difference in their physics? It is to be found in the Newtonian concept of inertia, the property of bodies to persevere in their states of rest or of uniform motion in straight lines as long as no net external forces act upon them.

Galileo and Newton never observed motions which conform to this concept. They are idealized states of affairs envisioning which led to the concept of inertia, the cornerstone of Newtonian physics. Had Newton been as austere an empiricist as

[16]Skinner, *B. F. D.,* p. 5.

[17]For an illuminating discussion of Aristotle's treatment of motion, see Stephen S. Toulmin's *Foresight and Understanding,* Harper & Row, N.Y., 1963.

Aristotle and Skinner, he could only have produced a sterile and feeble science. All this is familiar to students of history and philosophy of physics. It is amazing, then, that Skinner over-looks the role of theoretical concepts and entities in physics and tells us that physics has become a great science by ignoring them and concentrating exclusively on the observable. He claims to follow and exhorts others to follow such a path toward a science of behavior. He may follow this path if it pleases him but it is false to assert that it is the method of physics.

What kind of a science of behavior results on Skinner's methodological prescriptions which reject theoretical concepts, mediating variables, and hypothetical states? Let us pursue this question through the following considerations: Suppose an organism O when presented with a stimulus S emits a response R. It makes sense to ask why O emits R rather than some other response, say $R^1$. But how explain this fact? What does it mean to explain it? It is useless and unilluminating to say that someone has conditioned O to so respond to S. But before dealing with this point of conditioning, let us ask why an organism which is not conditioned in the laboratory gives a particular response to a particular stimulus. It does not help much again to say that the organism has been conditioned by its environment to so respond.

Even if this is true, it is not senseless to press for an explanation of the fact that the organism, whether within or without the laboratory, emits a certain response to a certain stimulus. The point here is that insofar as Skinner refuses to go beyond merely observing that an organism responds to a certain stimulus in a certain way, he cannot offer an explanation of the fact that it does so. In order to explain it, one has to consider the structure and constitution of the organism as well as that of the stimulus. Then one can establish causal links between S through O to R. But to take into account the structure and constitution of the organism is to go beyond the molar (overtly observable) level into the molecular, atomic, electronic, and neurophysiological levels and at these levels one cannot avoid theoretical concepts, entities, mediating variables, states, and processes of physics, chemistry, biology, and neurophysiology. But Skinner mocks at physiological psychology when he writes

"... many physiological psychologists continue to talk freely about states of mind, feelings, and so on, in the belief that it is only a matter of time before we shall understand their physical nature."[18] Not only is this a caricature of physiological psychology but implicit in it is the conviction that physiological psychology can throw no light on the so-called states of mind and feelings.

It is worth noting that Skinner does not offer any arguments in support of this conviction. May it not be that it is merely his wish that the science of behavior not be usurped by physiological psychology? Be that as it may, physiological psychology, if it uses terms such as 'states of mind' and 'feelings,' it is not with the belief that there are some ultimate entities denoted by them but only as terms belonging to the common fund of our vocabulary and with the aim of correlating them with physiological terms. Thus when someone says that he feels pain, the physiological psychologist tries to find out the physiological events and states associated with feeling pain. Similarly, he would like to determine the physiological states correlated with thinking, dreaming, learning, being aggressive, being hungry, sexually excited, depressed, etc. Part of the aim of neurophysiology, then, is to explain and account for phenomenological states in terms of neurophysiological, physico-chemical concepts. But by rejecting physiology as inappropriate to the study of behavior Skinner is unable to explain the observed S-R correlations. In this manner, then, the S-R correlations are left as either mysterious or as not needing any explanation. In spite of this lack of explanatory power on the part of his science of behavior, Skinner constantly talks about scientific analysis and explanation of human behavior. But if all one has are S-R correlations, what explains them? It is important to emphasize that physiological psychology can explain and predict behavior through correlations between phenomenological and physiological states without having to deny the subjectivity of experience.

I return now to the question of conditioning an organism O to emit a response R to a stimulus S. Skinner would say that

---

[18]Skinner, *B. F. D.,* p. 12.

the organism emits R to S because it has been conditioned to so respond. But we want to ask: can the organism be conditioned to emit any arbitrarily chosen response to an equally arbitrarily chosen stimulus? I do not know how a radical behaviorist would respond to this question. But it is clear that a given organism cannot be so conditioned. Pigeons can be taught to play ping-pong but one can hardly hope to teach them how to play chess or do topology. One may be inclined to object to this by saying that it is an unfair and unreasonable question. But, I ask, why so? The obvious reply is that playing chess and doing topology are too complex activities to be taught to pigeons. But this only provokes us to ask further: What is meant by 'complex activities?' Well, the answer is that pigeons just do not have the kind of equipment needed to learn these activities. It is clear by now that our first question cannot be answered except by referring to the physiological structure and constitution of organisms and their range of potential for activities. The point here is that a genuine explanation as to what an organism can or cannot be conditioned to do has to take into account the structure and constitution of the organism, not just the environment. But Skinner tells us that we do not have to concern ourselves with what goes on under the skin for constructing a so-called science of behavior. To be sure, he does use such phrases as 'genetic endowment.'[19] But it seems to be purely a matter of courtesy or a vague reference to evolution insofar as he never spells out what 'genetic endowment' includes and what role it plays in determining specific behaviors of specific organisms.

Consider now the predictive power of Skinner's science of behavior. Let us consider again an organism O which has been so conditioned as to emit a response R to a stimulus S. The Skinnerian psychologist who conditioned the organism now says that he can predict the behavior of the organism as: whenever S then R. Now suppose O is presented with S but instead of R the organism has emitted a response $R^1$. Obviously, the prediction is falsified. But how explain this? The behaviorist can only say either that the schedules of reinforcement are not appropriate

---

[19]Skinner, *B. F. D.*, p. 11.

and adequate or simply that the conditioning has not been successfully accomplished. Let us condition O further under appropriate schedules. Suppose now that S is presented and the organism does emit the response R. What does this prove? It proves no more than that the conditioning is successful. But we can still ask: Why does O now emit R for S? The behaviorist's answer is obvious: "Well, we have conditioned it to so emit." I submit that in truth there can be no question of prediction in Skinner's approach to psychology in any sense resembling that in physics. Genuine prediction arises only when one can predict what response would be emitted by an organism when presented with a certain stimulus. In physics one talks about prediction in precisely this sense. Thus take, for example, the simple problem of predicting where a projectile shot in a certain direction with a certain speed would hit the ground. The physicist starts out with some general laws, links them with certain initial conditions, and logically deduces from this conjunction the prediction. This procedure for constructing explanations and predictions is an instance of what in philosophy of science is known as the 'hypothetico-deductive method.' Skinner's methodology does not permit such predictions. The reason for this is simple: Skinner's science of behavior does not have any general laws, such as the law of gravitation, the laws of motion, or Maxwell's laws of electromagnetism. All it has, and can ever hope to have, are simple inductive generalizations contingent upon conditioning. And most of these are plain common sense, such as a man deprived of food will be hungry and would display the behavior of "looking for food" and on finding it behaves in a certain manner. Thus the confirmation of a prediction of the kind "whenever S, then R" is at best a confirmation of a contingent (upon conditioning) inductive generalization. No wonder, Skinner's supposed science of behavior can never hope to have explanatory and predictive power. It can neither explain the observed S-R correlations nor predict the behavior of an organism in any sense other than the trivial and obvious fact that it has been conditioned. In order to drive this point home further, I quote Professor Wisdom. Thus, commenting on C. L. Hull's behaviorism, which has many important features in common with that of Skinner's, Wisdom writes:

... To many it is a sign of scientific achievement and meta-scientifically satisfactory to find that a theory leads to known facts. This can be true, but also can be a major delusion. Certainly a theory should do at least this much, but if it does no more it is not a serious theory. To aim at mere conformity with the evidence is one of the subtler and rarer misuses of the hypothetico-deductive system. It is felt intuitively that a good theory must accord with reality. This is, of course, true in the sense that its consequences must accord with observation; but such accordance provides no corroboration if the consequences are to be expected in any event—if they are also consequences of other accepted theories or if they are simply matters of common experience. Only if they are not to be 'naturally' expected, does the theory conflict with existing knowledge. Now Hull does not treat these theorems [which he claims to derive from his hypothetico-deductive system], which express what is already known, as a mere preliminary condition for having a satisfactory theory, before going on to serious work; he treats them as substantial results. Thus Hull's theory seems to lack *novelty-producing power* in that it *lacks consequences that conflict with existing knowledge.* [20]

I now consider the problem of conditioning an organism O to emit a response R to a stimulus S and subsequently changing its conditioned pattern of behavior. Let us start with an organism O that has been conditioned to emit a response R to a stimulus S. Now suppose that we wish to draw a response $R^1$ from the organism to the same stimulus. How does a radical behaviorist go about accomplishing this? Note that he has nothing to go by except what is observable. If so, the only way open to him is to erase the previous conditioning and recondition the organism so as to make it emit the response $R^1$ to the stimulus S. But if one is willing to consider the structure and constitution of the organism, one does not have to go through the process of erasing the previous conditioning and therewith the previous pattern of behavior. All one needs to do is to produce changes in the physiology of the organism. Schematically, this may be expressed as follows: Initially S-O-R expresses the causal links from S through O to R. Since Skinner ignores the O-component, he has to erase the old S-R and establish the new $S-R^1$. In contrast, the physiological psychologist, by altering

20J. O. Wisdom, *op. cit.*, p. 137.

the conditions in O, can readily obtain S-O-R[1]. To put it differently, the organism is not an empty black box with gods and demons inhabiting it; rather, the organism is a dynamic physiological matrix on which depend the range and quality of its responses to stimuli. By manipulating this matrix, we can make the organism emit *different responses to the same stimuli.* Not only that; we can also make the organism emit *the same response to different stimuli.* Thus, for example, a satiated animal can be made to eat as if he were hungry and, conversely, a hungry and starved animal can be made to behave as if he does not even notice the food in his presence.[21]

It is well-known that chimpanzees are mortally afraid of snakes. But when certain operations are performed on their brain, they display no panic at the sight of snakes.[22] All these experiments in neurophysiological psychology show that behavior of organisms is not simply the result of arbitrary and capricious conditioning. It has roots deeper in the physiological makeup of the organism, the understanding of which makes it possible not only to describe but also to explain and control behavior. But if one ignores physiology and limits oneself to overt behavior, as the radical behaviorist does, one can neither explain nor predict behavior; all one can do is to describe and control behavior in a limited domain. It is worth pointing out here that Skinner's phrase *"relation* between behavior and the environment"[23] is puzzling. It is puzzling because it is not behavior that interacts and is related to the environment. Behavior *is* the interaction and relation between the organism and environment. How was Skinner led to such a senseless locution? Such locutions are a direct consequence of a conception of science which pretends to study the behavior of an organism by ignoring the organism altogether.

---

[21]"The Biology of Behavior," in *Biology and the Future of Man,* ed. Philip Handler, Oxford University Press, N.Y., 1970, p. 400.

[22]See Dean E. Woodbridge's *The Machinery of the Brain,* McGraw-Hill, N.Y., 1963; as well as his *Mechanical Man,* McGraw-Hill, 1966.

Jose M. R. Delgado, *Physical Control of the Mind,* Harper & Row, N.Y., 1969.

J. C. Eccles, *The Neurophysiological Basis of Mind,* Oxford University Press, N.Y., 1953.

[23]Skinner, *B. F. D.,* p. 15.

Skinner constantly confuses control of behavior with explanation and prediction of behavior on the one hand and technology with science on the other. One can and does control the behavior of organisms, including man, without necessarily being able to explain it. It is one thing to train, say, a rat or a chimpanzee, to perform certain tasks, for example, pressing a lever or riding a bicycle, and quite another to explain, apart from the trivial and obvious assertion that someone conditioned or trained it, how and by what mechanisms the organism behaves as it does under certain conditions. Animal-trainers and circus people have certainly achieved amazing results in the area of controlling the behavior of animals. But it would be absurd to say on that account that they have provided a scientific explanation of the behavior of their trainees. But then those humble animal-trainers never pretended to be forging a science of behavior by coining such phrases as 'operant conditioning,' 'reinforcement,' and 'schedules of reinforcement.' They did whatever they found necessary for successfully getting an animal to perform certain tasks. Nor could one claim that only Skinner and his followers but not the ordinary animal-trainer and circus people were successful in training and controlling animals. Why, then, were these latter not hailed as behavioral scientists as Skinner and the radical behaviorists were? Any local dog-trainer is as astute and successful, if not more, as Skinner is in training animals. And if Skinner is recognized as a behavioral scientist, then, to be fair, the unlettered and unsung animal-trainer also deserves that appellation. The point of these remarks is that controlling behavior is very different from explaining it; and neither Skinner nor his non-academic counter-parts have explained behavior although they have some success in the control of behavior:

> Conditioning is a specific form of behaviorism. Behavior-
> ism is the study of bodily movements, the 'outside' of an event
> the only things 'observable' and 'scientific.' Add to this the
> restriction of inertness, for it is natural enough to link
> dynamism with the inside, and we get a set-up for laws of
> behavior of a conditioning type. This is the Weltanschauung
> that owes its inspiration to Pavlov. The sort of behavior and the
> sort of laws that do appear to satisfy this framework are
> party-line reactions and propaganda, or reaction-patterns and

pain-inductance. Such activities are possible and can be carried out effectively ... *they are standard for house-training puppies and kittens.* [24]

By way of explanation, neither Skinner nor the animal trainer can say anything more than "Well, the animals behave the way they do because we have trained them to behave so," which in any case is obvious but is no explanation at all. Explanation of behavior can only come from an effort to establish causal links between a stimulus through the organism to the response. Only then can one be said to understand behavior, not when one is merely able to control it. The Romans who built colossal buildings that lasted a long time cannot be said to have a science of building in comparison with the modern engineer. People have been doing all kinds of things from time immemorial but that it is the case is not to be thought of as their having a scientific explanation of what they have been doing, no matter how successfully. Otherwise, we would be compelled to say that the primitive cave-dweller who successfully made fire and the Australian aborigine who has been effectively using the boomerang are scientists par excellence. To the contrary, only when one understands the phenomenon of fire and the flight of the boomerang can one be said to have a science of fire and the boomerang.

I now want to ask whether Skinner's claim that "it is a long-standing conviction that for much of human behavior there are no relevant antecedents" is true. It is surprising that Skinner manages to overlook the fact that the problem of determinism-versus-freedom is one of the oldest in the history of philosophy, both Eastern and Western. Put briefly, it is the problem whether man's behavior is determined by forces and factors on which he has no control or is the result of his own freedom. I am not saying that this problem has been solved by philosophers and psychologists long ago. All that needs to be stressed at the moment is that it is simply false to say that people hitherto never even entertained the possibility that human behavior is determined by relevant antecedent events and circumstances. The very fact that philosophers since Epicurus and Lucretius

---

[24]J. O. Wisdom, *op. cit.,* p. 139 (emphasis added).

through Leibniz, Spinoza, and Kant discussed this problem with great dialectical subtleties shows that, contrary to Skinner's assertion, men were not only aware of the problem but treated it from different points of view and proposed different solutions. We need not concern ourselves here with the correctness or otherwise of their solutions. Suffice it to point out that some argued that man's behavior is strictly determined by antecedent conditions, others that man is wholly free, and yet others that he is partly determined and partly free.

It is important to note that the problem of determinism-versus-freedom is a metaphysical problem and hence is not solvable by empirical-scientific methods. That is, any proposed solution of it is not open to empirical check. Even today philosophers are fiercely battling each other on this problem. Rejecting the autonomous man (who is thought to be free and hence whose behavior uncaused), Skinner asserts that all behavior is reaction to stimuli.[25] Skinner, in order to support this general claim concerning behavior, should therefore show that all behavior is the product of environment. This is not, I remind the reader, a distortion of Skinner's thesis; nor is the demand that he vindicate his thesis irrelevant. For Skinner's rejection of the so-called inner man, another name for the autonomous man, and the freedom claimed for him by the libertarians logically requires that Skinner justify his universal claim that *all* behavior is determined and conditioned by the environment. In the absence of such a justification, Skinner's claim can only be regarded as a metaphysical dogma and not a verifiable scientific proposition. But, equally, that such a justification is lacking does not prove the contrary, namely, there is an inner man endowed with freedom. Put differently, both Skinner's thesis of universal determinism and its antithesis of universal freedom are metaphysical theses beyond the pale of science. The choice between the two is simply a matter of one's philosophical outlook, weltanschauung, and extrascientific biases and commitments. To be sure, proponents of each thesis offer in support of it their own arguments purported to be scientific. Thus Skinner's supposed arguments, if any, for universal determinism and be-

---

[25]Skinner, *B. F. D.*, p. 18.

haviorism are no more than rationalizations of his prior commitment to a certain point of view and there is nothing about his thesis that could be resolved by empirical-scientific methods, notwithstanding claims by Skinner to the contrary that his thesis of universal behaviorism is based on scientific analysis.

It should also be emphasized that for Skinner the autonomous man is not only scientifically irrelevant but is a myth. This is an ontological claim in that it asserts that there *cannot exist* entities and states of certain kinds. But nowhere does Skinner even so much as hint how to go about determining the truth of this assertion. Disappointingly enough, all he gives us are rhetoric and propaganda. And one wonders since when these have become part and parcel of 'scientific analysis.' It is worth reminding the reader that a lack of proof against the existence of the autonomous man does not constitute a proof of his existence.

Skinner talks about new evidences of the predictability of human behavior.[26] But how and where in his S-R paradigm can the question of prediction arise in a non-trivial way? As has been pointed out earlier, insofar as Skinner rejects theoretical concepts and hypothetical entities, he cannot even talk about predicting behavior in any sense other than the dog-trainer's prediction of the behavior of his conditioned animal. It is also interesting that Skinner does not produce any examples of the new evidences he claims.

Insofar as Skinner could not demonstrate his central thesis, namely, universal determinism and behaviorism, his assertion to the effect that freedom, dignity, and worth of man are fictions is also undemonstrated, for affirming freedom, dignity, and worth is, on Skinner's own admission, logically equivalent to affirming the autonomous man, which in turn is logically equivalent to the denial of universal determinism.

Before closing this chapter, I wish to examine some of Skinner's charges against what he calls "traditional explanations of behavior." Let us take the first charge: "We are told that to control the number of people in the world we need to change people's *attitudes* toward children, . . ."[27] What precisely is wrong with this way of speaking? I take it that Skinner's point

---

26Skinner, *B. F. D.*, p. 21.
27*Ibid.*, p. 9.

in italicizing 'attitudes' is that people who use this phrase really believe that there are certain entities called 'attitudes,' 'pride,' 'sense of reponsibility,' etc. which are to be changed in order to control the number of people in the world. I suggest that Skinner take a close look at what people who talk in these phrases actually do to change attitudes. Surely, it would be absurd to say that they go about looking for attitudes, pride, and sense of responsibility in basements, closets, heads, and hip-pockets. They may engage in discussions producing relevant facts and figures, convincing others of the advantages of a small family and the burdens of a large family. And if at the end of such discussions and debates a man who was initially in favor of a large family is persuaded to change his position, to have a small family, and in turn to engage in argument and discussion with others and bring them to accept in theory and practice population control measures, then one is said to have changed the attitude of another. To be sure, different people adopt different techniques and means of persuasion, some effective and others ineffective.

Does Skinner have radically different means of changing attitudes? I cannot see what is so different that he suggests apart from rewards to induce change. But there is nothing new about this method of rewards. The government of India has been doing everything from large-scale propaganda and free distribution of contraceptives to giving cash rewards to people who undergo birth control operations (free of charge). What is it, then, that Skinner does which ordinary people do not know? What is it that his supposed science of behavior does which folk wisdom does not know? Be that as it may, the point here is that the fact that people employ such phrases as 'attitudes,' 'pride,' etc. does not mean that they believe that these terms refer to some ghostly entities lurking under one's skin. These expressions are part and parcel of our common vocabulary facilitating communication. To charge people who use such terms with believing in the existence of some mentalistic entities is totally unfounded and can only serve as a basis on which to set up strawman arguments, and that is precisely what Skinner does in order that he may claim that his science of behavior is something profound and radically different from common sense and folk wisdom.

Similar remarks apply to his other strawman examples. Yes, these ways of talking are indeed 'staple fare.'[28] But it is also staple fare that those who talk in these terms do not believe there are entities called alienation, hopelessness, frustration and go on a hunt for them on weekends. It is indeed true that "there is nothing like it in modern physics or most of biology,"[29] because physics does not deal with frustrated electro-magnetic fields, disaffected difraction patterns, the death instinct of deuterons, or the masochism of mesons; nor biology with the belligerence of bloodcells, the collective hatred of chromosomes, the repression of RNA, or the depression of DNA. Even as shorthand ways of referring to the observable behavior of these physical and biological entities, these phrases are inappropriate and absurd. But in the field of human behavior such phrases are perfectly sensible insofar as they are abbreviations for observable behavior. By the way, it should be of interest to Skinner to know that there are some laws and principles in physics, such as Fermat's principle of least time and Gauss' principle of least action, which are couched and interpreted in a teleological language, although it is required that these principles be given unique mathematical-dynamical formulations.[30] The fact that these are often expressed in a teleological language does not, however, mean that physicists believe that light and physical systems have purposes and wills. Insofar as such principles enable the physicist to describe, explain, and predict the behavior of relevant phenomena, they have a place in physics.

[28]Skinner, *B. F. D.*, pp. 9-10.

[29]*Ibid.*, p. 10.

[30]Henry Margenau, The Nature of Physical Reality, McGraw-Hill, N.Y., 1950, pp. 422-424.

... But physical science also contains laws which are expressed as integral equations, and these can be regarded as the modern carriers of the Aristotelian final cause, now called purpose.... By means of a trick well known to mathematicians (finding the integral a minimum or a maximum) he converts the integral relation into a set of differential equations called Lagrange's equations, and these are of the causal type. He has thus—this may come as a shock to metaphysicians—*transformed a purpose into a cause.* [Fermat's principle of least time, Gauss' principle of least constraint, the principle of least action, and Hamilton's principle are examples of what an Aristotelian may want to regard as teleological principles in nature].

It is also interesting, if not comical, to note that while Skinner vehemently protests against the use of mentalistic and teleological language in describing human behavior, he himself freely and liberally employs such language but with the apology that

> The text will often seem inconsistent. English, like all languages, is full of prescientific terms which usually suffice for purposes of casual discourse. No one looks askance at the astronomer when he says that the sun rises or that stars come out at night, for it would be ridiculous to insist that he should always say that the sun appears over the horizon as the earth turns or that the stars become visible as the atmosphere ceases to refract sunlight.... The use of casual expressions is much more likely to be challenged.... No doubt many of the mentalistic expressions imbedded in the English language cannot be as rigorously translated as 'sunrise,' but acceptable translations are not out of reach.[31]

In other words, Skinner reserves for himself the right and privilege to use casual expressions but denies others similar rights and privileges; and when they use such expressions, he does look askance at them and ridicule them as believing in mysterious entities such as alienation, frustration, and anxiety. This once again confirms how desperately Skinner needs fictions to kick around and thereby show us the alleged power and clarity of the pretentious translations of his science of behavior. Skinner's charge that people who talk and write in mentalistic and teleological language believe in the existence of strange and ghostly entities would have a stronger case had he conducted an empirical inquiry, such as a poll, to determine how many of those people actually believe so. He could have discovered by an empirical investigation, for example, what people mean by 'attitude' and what they actually do when they say they are trying to change someone's attitude. But armchair psychology and philosophy come easier than empirical investigation, which will only gobble up the precious myths one so badly needs in order to present one's own dogma in a favorable light.

---

[31]Skinner, *B. F. D.*, pp. 23-24.

# Chapter III

## BEHAVIORAL ANALYSIS OF VALUES

One of the most persistent and vexing problems in the history of philosophy is that of values in general and of ethics and morality in particular. Ever since his ascent to the stage of reflective thought, man has been confronted with the questions: What is good? What is right? What is wrong? How ought I to conduct myself with other men, individually and collectively? Are good and bad and right and wrong—morality and value— purely relative or are they absolute? Thinkers from Socrates down to Bertrand Russell have wrestled with these questions with the hope of finding answers as guides to human conduct. But, unfortunately, there has been no agreement to date on solutions to these issues and problems. Thus while some argued for moral and value absolutism, others held that morality and values are purely relative, and yet others maintained that the whole problem of ethics and values is unsolvable, in that against every supposed solution one can pit a counter-solution. In particular, absolutism in its various forms proved extremely vulnerable and many maintained that at bottom absolutism is merely a dogma which cannot be rationally justified. All that can be said in support of any ethical position, it has been argued, is that it is expedient, useful, subscribed to by the majority, etc. In fact, the logical positivists have gone so far as to claim that ethical and value statements are not statements capable of being true or false.[32] Despite their striking grammatical resemblance to statements which are capable of being true or false, moral and value statements are in fact disguised

---

[32]A. J. Ayer, *Language, Truth, and Logic*, Dover Publications, Inc., N.Y., 1946, Ch. VI.

imperatives and exhortations, which can only be obeyed or disobeyed (or accepted or rejected) but cannot be true or false. Some have therefore called them 'pseudo-propositions.' Further, according to the positivists, when an ethical dispute is carefully analyzed, it becomes clear that the disputants are not really disagreeing about facts but about their attitudes and commitments. No wonder, then, no amount of factual evidence and data concerning an issue can resolve the ethical dispute unless somehow or other, by persuasion, rhetoric, threat, or authority, the attitude of one or the other of the antagonists is changed. That is, change in attitude is a necessary condition for the resolution of an ethical dispute. But, one may wonder, how is it that there has been so much controversy about values and morality when it is transparently clear to everybody what is good, bad, right, and wrong.

In order to explain the unresolvable nature of value and ethical conflicts, let us start with the fundamental dichotomy of statements in this context. Philosophers have divided, for purposes of discussion of ethics and values, statements into two broad classes: the descriptive and the normative. A descriptive statement is one which affirms or denies a state of affairs, actual or possible. Thus "there is a cat on the mat," "metals conduct electricity," "the moon is a quarter of a million miles from the earth," and "two-headed men inhabit Neptune" are examples of descriptive statements. The distinguishing feature of descriptive statements is that they are in principle open to empirical verification. It is not necessary, however, for a statement to have been actually verified in order that it may be called 'descriptive.' All that is required is that it be, in principle, verifiable. Thus the statement "two-headed men inhabit Neptune," although not yet shown to be true or false, is open for such determination. We know what we should do in order to verify this statement, in the sense that we can unambiguously specify what operations are to be performed to determine whether or not it is true. It is implicit that the operations to be performed should not violate any laws of nature known at the given time. On the other hand, we have normative statements such as "one ought not to steal" and "thou shalt not commit murder." The characteristic feature of normative statements is that they set forth norms or standards of behavior.

Although it is not clear whether normative statements have any descriptive content, even those who say that they do maintain that their unique feature is non-descriptive and normative and hence are not in principle translatable into purely descriptive statements. It is important to note that some purely descriptive statements may contain normative statements as parts. Thus "in tribe T of Uganda stealing is wrong" is descriptive, in that it is determinable as being true or false. It is irrelevant whether or not one agrees with tribe T's conception of wrongness. All one needs to know is tribe T's conception of wrongness in order to determine whether tribe T regards stealing as wrong. Cultural anthropology abounds in statements of this kind. Be that as it may, what is important for our purposes is to note that normative statements are not exhaustively translatable into descriptive statements. Thus consider the statement "you ought to tell the truth." According to a major school of contemporary philosophy, this statement is to be understood as "I approve of telling the truth; do so as well."[33] The hearer may abide by these injunctions or violate them. Whatever the case may be, one thing is certain: there can be no doubt that there are descriptive and factual statements on the one hand and normative statements on the other, with a gulf between the two. The Scottish philosopher David Hume stated about two centuries ago that the gap between 'is' and 'ought' is a logical gap which cannot be bridged.[34] Put differently, Hume proclaimed that it is impossible to derive a normative statement from factual statements. The German philosopher Immanuel Kant also recognized such a gap when he excluded morality from the realm of pure reason and relegated it to that of practical reason. Even Bertrand Russell, the most passionate activist in human affairs, concluded thus:

> Ethical argument, when it is not merely as to the best
> means to a given end, differs from scientific argument in being
> addressed to the emotions, however it may be disguised by the

[33]C. L. Stevenson, *Ethics and Language,* Yale University Press, New Haven, 1960, p. 22.

[34]Arnold A. Johanson, "A Proof of Hume's Separation Thesis Based on a Formal System for Descriptive and Normative Statements," to be published shortly in *Theory and Decision* provides a rigorous defense of Hume.

use of the indicative mood. It must not be supposed that, on this account, ethical argument is impossible; it is easy, if not easier, to influence emotions by argument as to influence intellectual convictions. The difficulty that will be felt is that, in intellectual argument, there is supposed to be a standard of impersonal truth to which we are appealing, while in ethics, on the above view, there appears to be no such standard. This difficulty is real and profound. [35]

Such, in brief, is the general philosophical position concerning the nature of ethics and values. To repeat, it is impossible to deduce an 'ought' statement from 'is' statements. No statements of value can be logical consequences of factual statements. Arguments in defense of this position will be presented in the sequel. In light of this background of the problem of values and ethics, I shall now examine Skinner's behavioral approach and solution to it.

Skinner acknowledges that there certainly is a problem of values. He says that as long as control of behavior is attributed to the so-called autonomous man, that notoriously elusive entity, people are happy and satisfied. But as soon as control of behavior is seen as exerted by external agent, one gets disturbed and upset and raises all kinds of questions and objections:

> Something is missing in this shift from internal to external control. Internal control is presumably exerted not only by but for autonomous man. But for whom is a powerful technology of behavior to be used? Who is to use it? And to what end? We have been implying that the effects of one practice are better than those of another, but on what grounds? What is the good against which something else is called better? Can we define the good life? Or progress toward a good life? Indeed, what is progress? What, in a word, is the meaning of life, for the individual or the species?
>
> Questions of this sort seem to point toward the future, to be concerned not with man's origins but with his destiny. They are said of course, to involve "value judgments"—to raise questions not about facts but about how men feel about facts, not about what man *can* do but about what he *ought* to do. It is usually implied that the answers are out of reach of science. Physicists and biologists often agree, *and with some justifica-*

[35]Bertrand Russell, *Human Society in Ethics and Politics,* Mentor Books, N.Y., 1962, p. 72.

*tion,* since their sciences do not, indeed, have the answers. Physics may tell us how to build a nuclear bomb but not whether it should be built. Biology may tell us how to control birth and postpone death but not whether we ought to do so. Decisions about the uses of science seem to demand a kind of wisdom which, for some curious reason, scientists are denied. If they are to make value judgments at all, it is only with the wisdom they share with people in general.[36]

Before going further, let us examine these observations. Thus if it is true, as Skinner himself admits, that physics and biology cannot answer value questions, since these sciences do not indeed have the answers ("with some justification"), then it is hard to understand Skinner's claim elsewhere that "We can follow the path taken by physics and biology by turning directly to the relation between behavior and the environment and neglecting supposed mediating states of mind,"[37] in forging a science of behavior. There seems to be an incompatibility between the two assertions: On the one hand that a science of behavior can be constructed by following the path of physics and biology and on the other that physics and biology cannot and do not have answers to value questions. In the face of such an incompatibility Skinner should admit that human problems, at least the ones dealing with values, are not amenable to solutions by the methods of physics and biology, and hence a science of behavior which claims to follow the path of physics and biology cannot hope to solve these problems but needs a unique and different method of its own. It is also not clear whether Skinner is saying that physics and biology *do not as of now* have answers to value questions or they *cannot* have them. But if physicists and biologists often agree, "and with some justification," that solutions to problems of value are out of reach of their sciences, then one wonders how Skinner as a behavioral scientist can hope to solve these problems with the methods paradigmatic of physics and biology. The inescapable conclusion seems to be that part of the science of behavior, that which deals with value problems, has to employ methods different from those of physics and biology. If so, Skinner's goal

---

[36]Skinner, *B. F. D.,* p. 102 (emphasis added).
[37]*Ibid.,* p. 15.

of a science of behavior in the image of physics and biology is nothing but a blissful dream. We might remind the reader here that it has been shown in an earlier chapter that Skinner's conception of the methods of physics and biology is a distortion of the actual methods of these sciences.

But, Skinner warns us,

> It would be a mistake for the behavioral scientist to agree. How people feel about facts, or what it means to feel anything, is a question for which a science of behavior *should* have an answer. A fact is no doubt different from what a person feels about it, but the latter is a fact also. What causes trouble, here as elsewhere, is the appeal to what people feel. A *more useful* form of the questions is that: If a scientific analysis can tell us how to change behavior, can it tell us what changes to make? This is a questions about the behavior of those who do in fact propose and make changes. People act to *improve* the world and to *progress toward a better way of life for good reasons*, and among the reasons are certain consequences of their behavior, and among these consequences are the things *people value and call good.*[38]

Let us now examine these remarks. We are told that what causes trouble here, as elsewhere, is the appeal to what people feel about facts. But Skinner says very little about the nature of this trouble and how exactly it is caused by appeal to what people feel about facts. I submit that the term 'trouble' is a value term in that what is regarded as trouble by one need not be so regarded by another. Something can be looked upon as trouble only in relation to some background assumptions and purposes. The sudden appearance of a policeman when someone is breaking into a home is trouble to the burglar but a boon to the home-owner. Skinner's reasons for regarding appeal to what people feel about facts as causing trouble can only be understood against his background assumptions as to what is to count as trouble. Appeal to feelings is troublesome for Skinner because he thinks that to admit feelings is to admit the inner man and his paraphernalia, such as mental states. Since Skinner a priori rules out the inner man as a fiction irrelevant to his science of behavior, it is only to be expected that he also regards appeals

---

[38]Skinner, *B. F. D.,* pp. 102-103 (emphasis added).

to feelings, which are traditionally attributed to the inner man, as troublesome. It would be interesting to ask whether the statement "How people feel about facts, or what it means to feel anything, is a question for which the science of behavior *should* have an answer"[39] is a fact or an appeal to Skinner's own feelings as to what a behavioral science should be. Following Skinner's own dictum that appeal to feelings is to be dismissed as irrelevant and troublesome, one can then tell Skinner to give us only facts and keep his feelings for himself.

Consider now Skinner's suggested alternative formulation of the question of value. The first thing to be pointed out here is that the term 'useful,' like 'trouble,' is a value term, in that something is useful to someone only from some specific point of view and for some purpose. Thus some people find religion useful and others not. Further, Skinner has yet to tell us what he means by *"improving* the world" and *"progress* toward a *better* way of life." It is worth noting that these expressions are dense with value terms. It is, to say the least, paradoxical that in a purported clarification of value terms and questions, Skinner employs value terms as clarificatory devices. Such clarifications are nothing short of pseudo-clarifications and question begging.

I come now to a detailed examination of Skinner's analysis of value terms and judgments in terms of behavioral criteria. He writes:

> Good things are positive reinforcers. The food that tastes good reinforces us when we taste it. Things that feel good reinforce us when we feel them. Things that look good reinforce us when we look at them.... (The things we call bad also have no common property. They are all negative reinforcers, and we are reinforced when we escape from or avoid them.)[40]

All this is tantamount to asserting that "X is good" means "X is positively reinforcing." Since Skinner recognizes *no other criteria* for calling X good or bad *than those of positive and negative reinforcement,* I am justified in saying that the following are Skinner's definitions of 'good' and 'bad': "X is good if and only if X is positively reinforcing" and "X is bad if and

[39]Skinner, *B. F. D.,* pp. 102-103 (emphasis added).
[40]*Ibid.,* pp. 103-104.

only if X is negatively reinforcing." This simply means that not only does Skinner assert that "If X is good then X is positively reinforcing" but also that "If X is positively reinforcing then X is good." A similar formulation results for "X is bad." It is not hard to refute this way of explicating 'good' and 'bad' by asking why a positive reinforcer is good. The only answer Skinner can give us is: because a positive reinforcer is good, which is really equivalent to asserting the tautology "A positive reinforcer is good because a positive reinforcer is good." Further, if "X is good" means "X is positively reinforcing," then, following G. E. Moore,[41] we can substitute "positively reinforcing" for "good" in "Good things are positively reinforcing" and obtain the tautologous and totally unilluminating assertion: "Positive reinforcers are positive reinforcers" as well as "good things are good things." One is then justified in charging Skinner with uttering tautologies and presenting them as genuine explications of ethical and value terms. In order to avoid such a charge, Skinner should admit that "X is good" is *not synonymous* with "X is positively reinforcing." But then he should tell us what precisely is the difference between the two sentences. It should be noted that, no matter what exclusively behavioral definition of 'good' is offered, for example, 'satisfying,' 'socially approved,' one can always assert without contradiction "X is satisfying and X is not good" and "X is socially approved and X is not good" as well as "X is good and X is not positively reinforcing" and "X is bad and X is not negatively reinforcing." But to admit that "X is good" cannot mean the same as "X is positively reinforcing" is to surrender the claim that value terms can be exhaustively explicated through behavioral terms. And unless and until Skinner shows us how to construct non-vacuous definitions of value terms exclusively through the concept of reinforcement, his assertion ". . . the reinforcing effects of things are the province of behavioral science, which, to the extent that it is concerned with operant reinforcement, is a science of values"[42] is at best rhetorical exhortation and at worst an empty and unwarranted claim.

---

[41]G. E. Moore, *Principia Ethica,* Cambridge Univ. Press, 1903.
[42]Skinner, *B. F. D.,* p. 104.

It is equally interesting to note that although Skinner complains that traditional, pre-scientific explanations of human behavior employ such objectionable terms as 'personality traits,' 'natures' and 'feelings,' he himself does not hesitate to use the term 'human nature' but quickly equates it with 'genetic endowment': "... it is part of the *genetic endowment called 'human nature'* to be reinforced in particular ways by particular things."[43] But he uses the term 'genetic endowment' whenever it suits his convenience without offering even an informal explication of the concept. Needless to say, the term means different things to different people. Without clarification, it is as handy and blanket an explanatory term as 'autonomous man.'

Consider now the statement: "Even as a clue, the *important* thing is not the feeling but the thing felt. It is the glass that feels smooth, not a 'feeling of smoothness.'"[44] The questions to ask here are, important for what? from what point of view? It is surely ambiguous to say that something is important without saying what it is important for and from what point of view. Or is there only one point of view? When Skinner says that the important thing is not the feeling but the thing felt, he is merely expressing his own preferences and not some truth about the world. One can assert, without sounding absurd or ridiculous, the contrary, that what is important is not the thing felt but the feeling. How is one to decide who is correct? It depends upon one's purposes and goals and as to what one wants to consider important. It should be noted further that even if Skinner tells us why and for what purposes he considers the thing felt and not the feeling as important, it does not follow that his assertion (that the thing felt is important) is true. Nor does it follow that everybody else *should* so consider the thing felt. Nor does it follow that Skinner has the right to condition others on the basis of his feelings and preferences that the thing felt and not the feeling is important.

Be that as it may, Skinner wants us to believe that people are so stupid as to believe that it is not the glass that feels smooth but "a feeling of smoothness" that feels smooth. I

---

[43]Skinner, *B. F. D.,* p. 104 (emphasis added).
[44]*Ibid.,* p. 107.

submit that this is another of Skinner's empty victories. Whoever has heard anyone say his feeling of smoothness feels smooth? In addition, there is a linguistic ambiguity here which Skinner exploits for his own purposes. The expression "it is the glass that feels smooth" is only the common way of saying, not that the glass feels smooth, but that someone feels the glass as smooth. But put in this way, it becomes clear that it is the person and not the glass that is the locus of feeling. But to acknowledge this to be the case, according to Skinner, would be to recognize the inner man, who does the feeling. Since Skinner a priori rejects the inner man, he has to shift the feeling to the glass through the expression "the glass feels smooth." Glasses *feel* neither smooth nor hard and no amount of linguistic subterfuge can eliminate the subject as the locus of feeling. Skinner also says ". . . we don't give a man pleasure or pain, we give him things he *feels* as pleasant or painful."[45] Whoever said that we give men pleasure or pain as we give them airplanes and avocadoes? Everybody knows what "giving pleasure or pain to others" means—people give each other things they feel as pleasant or painful. No man has ever given another a packet of pleasure as a Christmas gift. Why then does Skinner have to say the obvious as if it were some profound discovery? It is interesting to note that Skinner cannot avoid the term 'feel' even in his supposed scientific formulation of giving pleasure and pain. If so, it is appropriate to ask him to provide us with a *wholly behavioral* definition of the term 'feel.' I have not come across such a definition either in Skinner's own writings or those of his followers. From what we have said earlier about the non-translatability of theoretical terms into exclusively behavioral terms, it follows that the term 'feel' cannot be given a purely behavioral definition.

Consider now another of Skinner's assertions:

> A person does not act for the good of others because of a feeling of belongingness or refuse to act because of feelings of alienation. His behavior depends upon the control exerted by the social environment.[46]

---

45Skinner, *B. F. D.*, p. 107.
46*Ibid.*, p. 110.

This is a universal claim in that it allows for no exception. Thus *if* someone points to an instance of a behavior which seems to contradict the above thesis, Skinner would say that there *must really* be some control exerted by the social environment which we are unable to detect. One is expected to take such a question-begging answer as true. The point here is that Skinner's thesis that all behavior is determined by environment is a universal thesis and is not open to refutation by any experience. It is much like the theological claim that God protects men. When we point to an instance of a man dying, the theologian tells us that God still protects him elsewhere. In short, nothing counts against the claim. It is so, not because it has been proven to be true universally, but because nothing like a proof can be offered and that one is simply committed to believing it, no matter what. Karl Popper has correctly classified such theses as metaphysical theses, in sharp contrast with scientific theses. Skinner's thesis above is a metaphysical thesis because it is about all behavior, not just this or that behavior, and hence rules out a priori any counter-example. It should be noted, however, that the claim that a particular behavior is determined by external environment is a genuinely empirical claim open to verification. But Skinner would not settle for a limited thesis. He wants a universal thesis and the high price he has to pay for it is its unverifiability in principle. That is, in asserting a universal, metaphysical, unverifiable thesis, Skinner is not, contrary to his claims, doing empirical science but expounding some pet dogmatic metaphysics.

I return now to a detailed examination of Skinner's behavioral treatment of the specifically ethical term 'ought.' Skinner admits that "'Should' and 'ought' begin to raise more difficult questions when we turn to the contingencies under which a person is induced to behave for the good of others."[47] He then offers a behavioral translation of "You ought to tell the truth" as follows' "If you are reinforced by the approval of your fellowmen, you will be reinforced when you tell the truth."[48] Consider now the case where a certain member of a certain tribe

[47]Skinner, *B. F. D.,* p. 112.
[48]*Ibid.,* p. 112.

X has witnessed his tribe commit an act of destruction on a neighboring tribe Y. Assume now this man has been caught and brought as a witness in a trial of his tribe. Obviously, the contingencies are such that if he tells the truth he will not only not win the approval of his tribe but incur its wrath and possibly suffer death. Thus if he wants to be reinforced by the approval of his fellowmen, he will be reinforced by telling untruth—that his tribe did not commit the alleged atrocities. In other words, our witness will be reinforced by the approval of his fellowmen, not by telling the truth but by telling the lie. This situation is a clear instance of the vulnerability of Skinner's translation "you ought to tell the truth" in terms of reinforcement. Put differently, Skinner's behavioral translation compels one to regard the most blatant lie as unblemished truth, insofar as the former produces, as in the present example, reinforcement by the approval of one's fellow men. Since Skinner permits *no other criteria than publicly observable behavior,* it follows that something is true insofar as it produces observable reinforcement by one's fellow men. Ex hypothesi, we are told by Skinner, there is nothing else for us to appeal to in order to know whether a man is telling truth than reinforcement by approval of his fellow men. Therefore, whatever produces reinforcement by the approval of our fellow men must be regarded as true. This is indeed a highly original and interesting theory of truth as well as of value judgments. In short, it is simply preposterous to say that truth is determined solely by the contingencies that control behavior and the attendant reinforcement. It is important to point out here that the terms 'reinforce' and 'reinforcement' have precisely defined meanings in the context of scientific discourse and laboratory training of organisms. The statement "you will be *reinforced* if you read *David Copperfield*" is senseless if 'reinforced' here is taken in the technical, scientific meaning. Needless to say, such senseless statements are the result of indiscriminately extending a precise scientific term from its domain of significant applicability to all cases and contexts. Skinner himself provides the meanings of 'reinforcer' and 'reinforcement' in the scientific context when he writes:

> A single instance in which a pigeon raises its head is a *response*. It is a bit of history which may be reported in any

frame of reference we wish to use. The behavior called "raising
the head," regardless of when specific instances occur, is an
operant. It can be described, not as an accomplished act, but
rather as a set of acts defined by the property of the height to
which the head is raised. . . . In the pigeon experiment, then,
food is the *reinforcer* and presenting food when a response is
emitted is the *reinforcement*. The *operant* is defined by the
property upon which reinforcement is contingent—the height to
which the head must be raised. The change in frequency with
which the head is lifted to this height is the process of *operant
conditioning.* [49]

Let the reader himself now analyze the statement "you will
be reinforced if you read *David Copperfield*" in order to
discover the inapplicability of 'reinforcement' here and therewith
the absurdity and senselessness of the statement.

Skinner continues by saying that

Once we have identified the contingencies that control
behavior called good or bad and right or wrong, the distinction
between facts and how people feel about facts is clear. How
people feel about facts is a by-product. [50]

But what does he mean by by-product? Is Skinner saying
that because he regards feelings as by-products, whatever he
means by the term, they are irrelevant to considerations of truth
and falsehood? Skinner's answer to this question is not at all
clear, for he says little besides proclaiming that feelings are
by-products.

In order to clearly bring out the supposedly crucial role of
supporting contingencies in matters of value, Skinner contrasts
his own analysis of value judgments with that of Karl Popper's
which Skinner describes as "a contrary traditional position." [51]
According to Popper,

In face of the sociological fact that most people adopt the
norm "Thou shalt not steal," it is still possible to decide to
adopt either this norm, or its opposite; and it is possible to
encourage those who have adopted the norm to hold fast to it,
or to discourage them, and to persuade them to adopt another

[49]B. F. Skinner, *Science and Human Behavior*, Free Press, N.Y., 1965, pp.
65-66.
[50]Skinner, *B. F. D.,* p. 113.
[51]*Ibid.,* p. 113.

norm. *It is impossible to derive a sentence stating a norm or a decision from a sentence stating a fact;* this is only another way of saying that it is impossible to derive norms or decisions from facts.[52]

Skinner criticizes Popper by saying that "The conclusion is valid only if indeed it is 'possible to adopt a norm or its opposite.'"[53]

I shall now show that Skinner's critique of Popper is unwarranted and unsupported. Skinner translates "Thou shalt not steal" (or equivalently, "You ought not to steal") as "if you tend to avoid punishment, avoid stealing," or "Stealing is wrong, and wrong behavior is punished."[54] "Such a statement," he adds, "is no more normative than if coffee keeps you awake when you want to go to sleep don't drink it."[55] It is worth noting that Skinner meticulously avoids putting the coffee example in its ought-formulation, which will read as "Thou shalt not drink coffee." The difference between this and "Thou shalt not steal" now becomes unmistakably clear. For one thing, when someone says the latter he is generally understood as saying "You shall not steal under any circumstances whatever," whereas "You ought not to drink coffee under any circumstances whatever" sounds both bizzare and absurd, unless the speaker happens to be the Chairman of the International Anti-Coffee Brotherhood. Further, there seems to be nothing specifically ethical about it, because the statement "coffee drinking results in sleeplessness" is empirically verifiable whereas it is not at all clear as to how to verify the statement "stealing is wrong." The coffee example is always tied down to some specific circumstances, while the ethical statements are usually intended by their speakers to be understood as not contingent upon any particular circumstances. Whoever has heard a moralist proclaim "Thou shalt not steal under certain circumstances" or "Thou shalt lie under certain circumstances?" The statement against drinking coffee is based on *purely* descriptive and

---

[52]Karl Popper, *The Open Society and Its Enemies,* Routledge & Kegan Paul, London, 1947, p. 53 (Skinner quotes this in *B. F. D.,* 113-114).

[53]Skinner, *B. F. D.,* p. 114.

[54]*Ibid.,* p. 114.

[55]*Ibid.,* p. 114.

empirical criteria, whereas "Stealing is wrong" is not so based and for that reason its meaning cannot be explicated in purely behavioral terms.

As has been pointed out earlier, 'wrong' is a value term and, no matter what behavioral translation of it is offered, onè can always without contradiction ask why is something wrong? Further, "Thou shalt not steal" is concerned with the relations of one man with another whereas "Thou shalt not drink coffee" is concerned with just one man. Moreover, there have always been men who do not steal even when there is no fear or threat of punishment. And if we were to accept Skinner's behavioral translation of "Thou shalt not steal" as "If you tend to avoid punishment, avoid stealing," then how is one to explain the fact that some men do not steal even when there is no threat of punishment? Obviously, Skinner would say that either there have been no such men or if there seem to be some, their refraining from stealing is still due to fear of punishment. But how does Skinner support the first alternative? The second alternative is not open to empirical check either, because it simply asserts that there must be fears and threats of punishment even when none are detectable and would even compel one to introduce such concepts as 'guilt' which are not translatable into purely behavioral terminology. I would like to see a behavioral scientist offer a fully operational definition of "X is suffering from guilt." It is important to note in this connection that the so-called lie-detectors work on the principle that the guilty man displays certain observable physiological effects under certain circumstances. But displaying such physiological effects is only a necessary but not a sufficient condition for pronouncing someone guilty; as is evident from the fact that some who were declared to be guilty on the basis of lie-detector tests were subsequently found to be innocent.

It is astounding that Skinner could be so naive as to believe that such a sophisticated logician as Popper could be unaware of the kind of trite and neat behavioral translations of value judgments which Skinner proposes. Such a belief shows that Skinner misses the whole point of Popper's claim that "It is impossible to derive a sentence stating a norm or a decision from a sentence stating a fact."[56] Popper does not deny the possibility of such translations as Skinner's. What he does deny is that there can be any *logical connections* between a normative statement and a factual statement. In other words, Popper maintains that there is an unbridgeable logical gap between facts and norms, between what is and what ought to be. If someone proposes a behavioral translation of a normative statement, it can be shown that the translation is a tautology. More specifically, Popper grants, for example, that stealing is punished is a fact, but denies the possibility of logically deducing "Stealing is wrong" from such a fact. Let me now illustrate the tautological character of Skinner's behavioral renderings of value judgments. Suppose A tells B "You ought not to steal," in Skinner's sense that "Stealing is wrong, and wrong behavior is punsihed." B would say: "Yes, I know stealing is punished. But I do not understand why on that account you want to call stealing 'wrong.' Please tell me why something for which one is punished is wrong." To which A could only reply: "Well, because it brings punishment," to which B would retort by saying "I know only too well from my experience that stealing brings punishment but I still want to know why for that reason you want to call it wrong." What more could A say? The full circle is now traversed: A can say no more than "anything that brings punishment is wrong because it brings punishment." The tautology is unavoidable as long as one, following the Skinnerian prescription, equates the value term 'wrong' with the descriptive phrase 'brings punishment.' No matter how long and how complex the proposed exclusively behavioral translation, one can always ask: Why is something with certain observable properties and consequences wrong? That is, one can assert without contradiction "X has the described observable properties and consequences but X is not wrong." Popper and other philosophers are fully aware of the various futile attempts to render value judgments into wholly descriptive, non-value statements. In the face of this fact, Skinner boldly comes forward with his simplistic translations as if they were some profound insight into the meaning of value judgments.

---

[56]Karl Popper, *op. cit.*, p. 53.

Skinner is equally mistaken in thinking that one cannot maintain the logical gap between facts and norms without necessarily subscribing to the notion of the autonomous man (or the ghost in the machine). There is no *logical connection* between belief in the autonomous man and the impossibility of deriving a normative statement from factual statements. The latter is a logical issue, not a pseudo-ontological issue concerning the autonomous man. Both the affirmation and denial of the autonomous man are *logically* compatible with the impossibility of deducing the ought from the is. Thus Skinner's objection that Popper's "conclusion is valid only if indeed it is 'possible to adopt a norm or its opposite',"[57] has nothing whatever to do with Popper's assertion concerning the logical impossibility of obtaining normative statements from factual statements. Popper makes it quite clear that "it is *possible* to encourage those who have adopted the norm to hold fast to it, or to discourage them, and to persuade them to adopt another norm."[58] That is, Popper grants that we can change the beliefs and behavior of people with respect to matters of value. But he also insists that this should not mislead one into thinking that there can be *logical connections* between factual and normative statements. It is therefore simply absurd to attribute to Popper belief in the autonomous man in order that he may advance the thesis of the impossibility of logically obtaining the ought from the is.

One final point: Kant distinguishes between what he calls "hypothetical and categorical imperatives." A statement such as Skinner's "if you want to avoid punishment, avoid stealing" is an example of the former, because avoiding stealing is governed by certain contingencies such as avoiding punishment. On the other hand, "Thou shalt not steal" is a categorical imperative, because it categorically (i.e., without qualification) asserts that "Thou shalt not steal, no matter what," not "If . . . then. . . ." Skinner might retort by saying that Kant is mistaken in interpreting ethical statements as categorical imperatives. But insofar as Skinner maintains that his is the only correct interpretation of ethical judgments, it follows that Skinner in effect is saying

---

[57]Skinner, *B. F. D.,* p. 114.
[58]Karl Popper, *op. cit.,* p. 53 (emphasis added).

that "Kant ought to have interpreted ethical statements in my manner" (or, better, "If Kant wants to avoid criticism by Skinner, Kant better accept Skinner's interpretation"). It should be clear by now that what Skinner is doing is not empirical science but the metaphysics of morals. He is pitting his own metaphysics of morals against that of Kant and other philosophers. Skinner has a world-view, according to which all behavior is the result of control exerted by the environment and categorical imperatives are senseless and smack of the autonomous man and hence should be rejected as unscientific and mythological. He is implicitly persuading others to accept his world-view and his theory of value. He is recommending that value judgments be treated as statements of contingencies and their effects. All this is dogmatic metaphysics and does not become science no matter how thickly disguised in the jargon of a pseudo-science.

# Chapter IV

## SKINNER ON THE EVOLUTION OF CULTURE

Having emphasized the crucial role of contingencies in interpreting ethical statements, Skinner proceeds to provide an account of the evolution of culture in terms of contingencies. He first takes objection to two anthropologists' observation that "the essential core of cultures consists of traditional (i.e., historically derived and selected) ideas and especially their attached values"[59] by saying:

> But those who observe cultures do not see ideas or values. They see how people live, how they raise their children, how they gather or cultivate food, what kinds of dwellings they live in, what they wear, what games they play, how they treat each other, how they govern themselves, and so on. These are customs, the customary *behaviors*, of a people. *To explain them we must turn to the contingencies which generate them.*[60]

Here, as elsewhere, Skinner's temptation to box with the strawman and the shadow is obvious. Thus he interprets the above anthropologists as having said that they *see* ideas and values, as one does cats and caterpillars. No anthropologist, or for that matter, nobody, believes that when he studies a culture he equips himself with some special device by which to observe ideas and values floating around the culture like moths and mosquitoes. What he observes are the behaviors of people, and by interpretation and inference he says that certain ideas and values are to be found in that culture in the sense that the

---

[59]Alfred L. Krober and Clyde Kluckhohn, "Culture: A critical Review of Concepts and Definitions," published in the *Harvard University Peabody Museum of American Archaeology and Ethnology Papers,* Cambridge, 1952, Vol. 47, No. 1.

[60]Skinner, *B. F. D.,* p. 60 (emphasis added).

behaviors observed seem to be based upon or guided by those ideas and values. But is Skinner unaware that this is the case? Surely not. Why, then, does he object to the above characterization of culture? Because Skinner holds and has been untiringly telling us that ideas and values are mentalistic entities, ghostly and fictitious, and hence should be banished from scientific analysis of any phenomenon, whether it is culture or behavior in general. It is for this reason that he presents the two anthropologists above as having claimed that they observe in a literal sense ideas and values.

Skinner's writings abound in this kind of shadowboxing and empty triumphs. Be that as it may, can Skinner do away with ideas? Consider someone reading Skinner's book. What is the behavior he is observing? Is he observing Skinner saying or doing something? One certainly observes some signs on a piece of paper, interprets them within a given linguistic framework and gathers what Skinner's ideas, views, values, and biases are, and anticipates on this basis how Skinner would behave in a given situation—for example, that he would reject and oppose any suggestion of the autonomous man (that he would deny human freedom), that he would be "positively reinforced" by people who agree with him, "negatively reinforced" by those who criticise him, etc. However all this may be, the question still is: Does anyone observe some behavior while reading a book? I am sure Skinner would consider such activities as reading and what is read as integral parts of our culture. If so, he has to tell us what it is that one observes, apart from the print marks, when one reads. It is pointless for Skinner to say that he is only concerned with reporting the observation that someone is reading. For this does not answer our question whether Skinner can recommend wholesale condemnation of ideas and still be able to say what behavior a man observes when he reads. I can only hope that Skinner's unmitigated zeal for an ill-conceived science of behavior would not drive him to the absurd reply that the man is observing the behavior of print marks. Notice that if we accept Skinner's notion of observing culture (as observing nothing but some behavior or other), no one can learn anything about a culture by reading, for it is indeed true that while reading one does not observe any behavior.

Skinner says that

> A culture, like a species, is selected by its adaptation to an
> environment: to the extent that it helps its members to get
> what they need and avoid what is dangerous, it helps them to
> survive and transmit the culture.[61]

Further,

> ...The contingencies characteristic of a culture may not be
> adequately transmitted, so that the tendency to be reinforced
> by a given set of values is not maintained. The margin of safety
> in dealing with emergencies may then be narrowed or broad-
> ened. In short, the culture may grow stronger or weaker and we
> may forsee that it will survive or perish. The survival of a
> culture then emerges as a new value to be taken into account in
> addition to personal and social goods.... A culture evolves
> when new practices further the survival of those who practice
> them.[62]

Finally,

> ...When it has become clear that a culture may survive or
> perish, some of its members may begin to act to promote its
> survival. To the two values which, as we have seen, may affect
> those in a position to make use of a technology of behavior—
> the personal "goods," which are reinforcing because of the
> human genetic endowment, and the "goods of others," which
> are derived from personal reinforcers—we must now add a third,
> the good of the culture. But why is it effective? Why should
> people in the last third of the twentieth century care about
> what the people in the last third of the twenty-first century
> will look like, how they will be governed, how and why they
> will work productively, what they will know, or what their
> books, pictures, and music will be like? No current reinforcers
> can be derived from anything so remote. Why, then, should a
> person regard the survival of his culture as a "good?"[63]

Thus, basic to Skinner's analysis of culture are three values,
personal goods, goods of others, and good of the culture.
Skinner now proposes to answer the question as to why a
person should regard the survival of his culture as a good. I shall
first present his answer and then examine it.

---

[61]Skinner, *B. F. D.*, p. 129.
[62]*Ibid.*, pp. 128-129, 134.
[63]*Ibid.*, p. 134.

Consistent with his view that mentalistic concepts such as feelings have no place in a scientific analysis of behavior, Skinner asserts that

> It is no help, of course, to say that a person acts "because he feels concern for the survival of his culture".... And what a person feels about the survival of his culture will depend on the measures used by the culture to induce its members to work for its survival.... Nor is it any help to say that that someone suddenly gets the idea of working for the survival of a culture and transmits it to others. An "idea" is at least as difficult to explain as the practices said to express it, and much less accessible. But how are we to explain the practices?[64]

Along with feelings, intentions are rejected by Skinner in consonance with his conception of scientific explanation of human behavior. Accordingly, he writes:

> Much of what a person does to promote the survival of a culture is not "intentional"—that is, it is not done *because* it increases survival value.[65]

At this point, we are given the innocuous tautology that "a culture survives if those who carry it survive."[66] But one wonders how this constitutes an answer to the original question as to why a person should regard the survival of his culture as good. All Skinner said thus far by way of an answer is that if those who carry a culture survive, then the culture survives. But this is properly an answer to the question: How does a culture survive? but not to the question Skinner started out to answer. It is also interesting to note that while Skinner vehemently objects to the use of such words as 'feeling,' he freely uses 'intentional,'[67] thereby giving the impression that the latter can be given an exhaustively behavioral explication. It is also amusing to notice Skinner's heroic efforts to circumvent having to bring people into an explanation in any significant way. Thus it is not persons but *measures* used by a culture that induce its members to work for its survival.

---

64Skinner, *B. F. D.*, pp. 134-135.
65*Ibid.*, p. 135.
66*Ibid.*, p. 135.
67*Ibid.*, p. 108.

Let us move on now to a consideration of Skinner's further attempts to answer the question as to why a person should regard the survival of his culture as good. He writes:

> Institutions may derive effective reinforcers from events which will occur only after a person's death. They mediate security, justice, order, knowledge, wealth, health, and so on, only part of which the individual will enjoy. . . . The honors accorded the living hero outlast him as memorials. Accumulated wealth outlasts the accumulator, as does accumulated knowledge; wealthy men establish foundations under their names, and science and scholarship have their heroes. The Christian notion of life after death may have grown out of the social reinforcement of those who suffer for their religion while still alive. . . . The individual is not, of course, directly affected by any of these things; he simply gains from conditioned reinforcers used by other members of his culture who do outlast him and are directly affected.[68]

However, he immediately adds:

> None of this will explain what we might call a *pure concern* for the survival of a culture, but we do not really need an explanation.[69]

Skinner's bag of troubles is now wide open. He starts out with the aim of answering a question and after considering certain answers and rejecting them ends up by saying that the question does not really need an answer. It is important to note that although Skinner earlier rejected the answer in terms of "a person's feeling concern for the survival of his culture," he nonetheless uses the phrase "pure concern for the survival of a culture." But verbal maneuvers can only beguile the unwary. The maneuver here is to drop the phrase "a person feels concern" and replace it with "a pure concern." Skinner, however, admits that even in his new formulation the question cannot be answered. But what is the real reason why Skinner is unable to provide an answer to the question even in his supposedly austere and scientific formulation? The reason, I submit, is that the concept 'concern' cannot be given an exhaustively behavioral explication. Some kind of mentalism is

---

[68]Skinner, *B. F. D.*, pp. 135-136.
[69]*Ibid.*, p. 136 (emphasis added).

analytically built into the concept of concern as it is in that of feeling. Let Skinner try to give a purely behavioral definition of 'concern.' I suspect that Skinner is aware of the difficulties associated with translating 'concern' into exclusively behavioral vocabulary. But having insisted upon an unqualified rejection of mentalistic concepts, he finds himself unable to answer his question (as to why a person should regard the survival of his culture good) in wholly behavioral terms. He therefore concludes that the question needs no answer at all. Such, then, is the plight of a conception of science which is bent upon looking and smelling as hygienic as a hospital room.

But Skinner now explains why no explanation is needed at all and in so doing presents us with irrelevant observations and downright tautologies. Thus he says:

> ...Just as we do not need to explain the origin of a genetic mutation in order to account for its effect in natural selection, so we do not need to explain the origin of a cultural practice in order to account for its contribution to the survival of a culture. The simple fact is that a culture which *for any reason* induces its members to work for its survival, or for the survival of some of its practices, is more likely to survive. Survival is the only value according to which a culture is eventually to be judged, and any practice that furthers survival has survival value by definition.[70]

But one would like to ask how the question: Why should a person regard the survival of his culture as good? is related to that of origins of cultural practices. The analogy of the origin of genetic mutations is wholly irrelevant here. It would be appropriate if there is some question of origins in the original question. In other words, the main question is not about the origin of a cultural practice, contrary to what Skinner's analogy of the origin of genetic mutations would lead us to believe. What Skinner is really doing here is to push aside the basic question and look, as usual, for strawmen who could be easily knocked off or simply dismissed as irrelevant. I do not see how the question: Why should a person regard the survival of his culture as good? is equivalent to the question: What is the origin of a cultural practice? Having shifted our attention from the

---

[70]Skinner, *B. F. D.*, p. 136.

former to the latter, it is easy for Skinner to say that the question of the origin of a cultural practice is irrelevant to our accounting for its contribution to the survival of a culture. This is totally unilluminating as an answer to the first question, for it has nothing to do with it. It is a proper answer to the question: Does a given cultural practice, whatever its origins, contribute to the survival of a culture? What Skinner is in effect saying is that a man's concern for the survival of his culture contributes to the survival of his culture, which is an answer to the question: Does a man's concern for the survival of his culture contribute to the survival of his culture? It should be clear by now that Skinner regards a person's *concern* for the survival of his culture itself *as a cultural practice.* Only thus could he turn the original question into one of the origin of a cultural practice and easily dismiss it as not needing an answer at all. But it is incomprehensible as to what one could possibly mean by saying that *concern* for the survival of a culture is a cultural *practice.*

Skinner uses the term 'reason' in his statement "... The simple fact is that a culture which *for any reason* induces its members to work for its survival, or for the survival of some of its practices, is more likely to survive."[71] But according to his own dictum we should demand of him an exhaustively behavioral explication of this term. Needless to mention, 'reason' is an essentially mentalistic term and insofar as he does not even hint as to how to translate it into exclusively behavioral terms, Skinner has no right to use it in explaining to us why no explanation is needed of the question: Why should a person regard the survival of his culture as good?

But of all things he says in this context, the most interesting and amusing is the statement "... Survival is the *only* value according to which a culture is eventually to be judged. ..."[72] Although this statement is ambiguous in that it does not say what it is a culture is eventually judged to be (good or bad?), I take it from the context that Skinner means "judged to be good." But this has hideous implications. For one thing, insofar as survival is the *only* value according to which a culture is eventually to be judged (to be good), it follows that a

---

[71]Skinner, *B. F. D.,* p. 136

[72]*Ibid.,* p. 136 (emphasis added).

given culture which guarantees its own survival by wiping out other cultures through sheer military might must be judged to be good. After all, the culture has managed to survive by exterminating all other cultures which it deems as threats to its own survival. This conclusion is inevitable insofar as Skinner explicitly says that survival is the *only* value according to which a culture is eventually to be judged. It is not necessary to mention that such a conclusion is the direct consequence of a dogmatic value judgment. Thus Skinner is proclaiming his own dogmatic commitment to a value which he holds as unique ('only' above) and highest. Such a proclamation is not an empirical-scientific assertion capable of truth or falsehood. It is merely a value judgment, a commitment, a recommendation, and an exhortation. In its undisguised and naked version, it reads "Survival is the only value according to which a culture *ought* to be eventually judged." And one wonders how Skinner would translate it into his scientific language of reinforcements and contingencies.

Finally, the statement "...*any practice* that furthers survival has survival value by definition"[73] is trivial and tautologous. It is part of Skinner's explanation of why we do not really need an explanation of his original question. Notice that the unqualified "any practice" in the above quote also generates the hideous consequences pointed out earlier.

Skinner now considers the same question (why should a man regard the survival of his culture as good)? from specific angles when he writes:

> ...But how can it [a government] answer the question: "Why should I care whether my government, or my form of government, survives long after my death?... But what is its [a religion's] answer to the question: Why should I work for the long-term survival of my religion?... But what is its [an economic system's] answer to the question: "Why should I be concerned about the survival of a particular kind of economic system?"[74]

He then answers these questions by saying:

---

[73]Skinner, *B.F.D.,* p. 136 (emphasis added).
[74]*Ibid.,* p. 137.

The only honest answer to that kind of question seems to be this: "There is no good reason why you should be concerned, but if your culture has not convinced you that there is, so much the worse for your culture.[75]

But is this really an answer? Does Skinner expect us to take it seriously? I am afraid that it is nothing but a piece of desperate rhetoric densely packed with Skinner's *feelings* as to what *ought* to be considered as the value according to which a culture is eventually to be judged. Skinner has every right to feel that his culture has convinced him that there is good reason why he should be concerned about its survival. But it is patently absurd, on his own conception of explanation, to offer feelings as an explanation and answer. Such an answer may very well be an *honest* answer, whatever that means. But that does not make it scientific. Moreover, how does Skinner go about translating 'honest' into purely behavioral terms? Such an answer is nothing short of a pseudo-scientific philosophy crawling under the heavy burden of self-imposed restrictions, flowing from an a priori, dogmatic metaphysics as to what is to count as a science of human behavior.

It is all too clear throughout his book that Skinner wears both the immaculate white coat of the self-proclaimed thoroughly empirical scientist and the mantle of the prophet, moralist, and messiah. But he does not wear them one at a time but simultaneously, projecting that glorious image of the scientific messiah. There is nothing objectionable if someone wants to proclaim his values and weltanschauung. But if such proclamations are dressed up in a pseudo-scientific jargon and are pretended to be scientific propositions open to verification, then we certainly have a right to protest. Thus the pronouncement: "We can nevertheless point to many reasons why people *should* now be concerned for the good of all mankind"[76] is a moral exhortation; or listen to the prophetic voice: "Both the species and the behavior of the individual develop when they are shaped and maintained by their effects on the world around them. *That is the only role of the future.*"[77] Neither of these is an

---

[75]Skinner, *B. F. D.*, p. 137.
[76]*Ibid.*, pp. 137-138.
[77]*Ibid.*, p. 142.

empirical-scientific statement. They belong in metaphysics and morals. But they are offered in the name of scientific analysis. One final point: Lest I be misunderstood as being intolerant of moral and metaphysical discourse, I wish to make it clear that I have nothing against such discourses, only against disguising them in obscure and pretentious terminology and offering them as a science in which, we are repeatedly told, there is no room for anything not directly observable. Let the reader ponder how he would empirically check, for example, the two statements quoted above.

# Chapter V

## SKINNER ON THE DESIGN OF CULTURE

In the present chapter, I shall examine Skinner's treatment of and solutions to the problems that arise in the design of culture. It will be shown that Skinner fails to face the problems squarely, and consequently much of what he proposes as solutions is either vague and dubious hints or rhetoric and crystal-gazing, having little or nothing to do with science.

Reiterating that goods are nothing but reinforcers and emphasizing the power of his scientific analysis (in sharp contrast with what he calls "personal experience and folk wisdom") for predicting and changing human behavior, Skinner says that most of the writings on cultural problems suffer from certain characteristic defects which explain our failure to deal adequately with these problems:

> No one knows the *best* way of raising children, paying workers, maintaining law and order, teaching, or making people creative, but it is possible to propose better ways than we now have and to support them by predicting and eventually demonstrating more reinforcing results. This has been done in the past with the help of personal experience and folk wisdom, but a scientific analysis of human behavior is obviously relevant. It helps in two ways: it defines what is to be done and suggests ways of doing it. How badly it is needed is indicated by a recent discussion in a news weekly about what is wrong with America. The problem was described as "a disturbed psychic condition of the young," "a recession of the spirit," "a psychic downturn," and a "spiritual crisis," which were attributed to "anxiety," "uncertainty," "malaise," "alienation," "generalized despair," and several other moods and states of mind, all interacting in the familiar intrapsychic pattern (lack of social assurance being said to lead to alienation, for example, and frustration to aggression). Most readers probably knew

what the writer was talking about and many have felt that he was saying something useful, but the passage—which is not exceptional—has two characteristic defects which explain our failure to deal with cultural problems: the troublesome behavior is not actually described, and nothing that can be done to change it is mentioned.[78]

Skinner then shows us how to translate the loose, vague, and predominantly mentalistic expressions into his precise scientific terminology, admitting nevertheless that the "paraphrases are too brief to be precise."[79] He claims that his scientific paraphrases "suggest the possibility of an alternative account, which *alone* suggests effective action."[80]

Skinner, without taking the trouble to find out what the writer of the allegedly unscientific and objectionable mentalistic statements means by them and how he would actually go about changing the situations he describes, wants us to believe that his own scientific translations reveal something profound of which the writer and his readers are ignorant as to both content and method. Thus, Skinner attributes to the man who says "X is dissatisfied or discouraged," the belief that certain entities called "discouragement" and "dissatisfaction" exist and presents him as one who launches a search for them in order that he may change X's state of discouragement and dissatisfaction. Nothing can be a greater makebelieve and more preposterous than this interpretation. Ask the man what he means and what he proposes to do in order to deal with what he regards as a problem situation. It is equally absurd to imply that the man who says that "X experiences an identity crisis" believes that there exists an entity called "identity crisis" which has to be captured in order that X's behavior may be understood and changed. Even the most belligerent and ardent mentalist has never been reported to have gone on a hunt after discouragement, dissatisfaction, frustration, guilt, and identity. Everybody knows, without needing Skinner's pretentious scientific analysis, that frustration, discouragement, dissatisfaction, identity crisis, etc. are descriptions of behavior. Thus when Mary Mut says that

---

[78]Skinner, *B. F. D.*, pp. 145-146.
[79]*Ibid.*, p. 147.
[80]*Ibid.*, p. 147 (emphasis added).

she has noticed this morning a bit of edginess in her boss, John
Angst, only someone eager for shadowboxing could understand
her as saying that she has noticed an entity called 'edginess'
floating about (in?) John. What she means is perfectly clear:
John's behavior this morning in a particular situation is different
in a specific manner from his normal behavior in that same
situation. On hearing Mary Mut, one does not ask her "How was
the edginess, round, square, red, or green?" but rather "Well,
what happened?" Neither she nor her hearer needs Skinner's
so-called scientific translations. Nor does it make sense to imply,
as Skinner certainly seems to, that Mary Mut thinks that John
needs to be treated for his edginess by the local witch doctor or
demonologist. When I say all this, I do not mean to imply for a
moment that everybody is a competent student of human
behavior and adept at changing and controlling it.

Certainly, the professional student of behavior, such as
Skinner, is able, by virtue of his training and practice, to locate
the antecedent events of a given piece of behavior by a
systematic study rather than by guesses and vague hunches and
thereby change and control behavior. But this does not mean
that the professional student of behavior has some deep insights
into the general principles of behavior beyond the ken of the
common man. In particular, the cornerstone of Skinnerian
behavior control, namely, people's behavior can be controlled by
rewards and punishments, is nothing new; if anything, it is as
old as man himself. Therefore, Skinner's accusation that people
believe in the existence of entities called 'anxiety' and 'aggression' is simply unfounded. Even those who believe in the
existence of souls do not seem to think that there are things
called 'frustration,' 'discouragement,' etc. Not even the notorious
Freudian analyst thinks that 'id,' 'ego,' 'super-ego,' and 'Oedipus
complex' denote some entities. He, too, attempts to understand
and change behavior by tracing it to antecedent events. That he
is often unsuccessful in his therapy does not mean that the
Freudian is a demonologist or necromancer chasing some
entities. Thus Skinner's claim that until the great science of
behavior came around no one knew that behavior is governed by
antecedent events and circumstances is a self-serving falsehood.
This is not to deny, however, that there have always been

believers in the hocus-pocus of the occult, but to accuse, as Skinner does, almost everybody of mystery-mongering and ignorance is wholly unjustifiable and amounts to no more than a triumph over the haystack and the cotton bale. To repeat, it is common knowledge and not some rare scientific insight that *"it is the contingencies which must be changed if his [anyone's] behavior is to be changed."*[81] That one talks freely in terms of mental states does not mean that in order to change and control behavior one conducts an assault on certain entities denoted by such terms. Quite the contrary, one attempts to change the conditions and events that determine the behavior describable through mentalistic phrases in an abbreviated fashion.

Skinner warns us against dismissing the

> frequent references to contingencies of reinforcement as a new fashion in technical jargon, but it is not simply a matter of talking about old things in new ways. Contingencies *are* ubiquitous; they cover the classical fields of intention and purpose, but in a much more useful way, and they provide alternative formulations of so-called 'mental processes.' Many details have never been dealt with before, and no traditional terms are available in discussing them. The full significance of the concept is no doubt still far from adequately recognized.[82]

It should be pointed out that besides merely asserting the obvious fact that contingencies are ubiquitous and that they cover the classical fields of intention and purpose in a more useful way, Skinner does not show in what way his so-called alternative scientific formulations are in principle different from what he contemptuously calls "folk wisdom." As pointed out earlier, no one, whatever may be his ontology of intention, purpose and mental processes in general, claims to change intentions and purposes by direct assault upon them. Rather, what one does is to change the events that led to the entertaining of a certain intention or purpose. Thus, for example, John's intention to kill his neighbor is based upon the former's belief that the latter is having an affair with John's wife. How does one go about changing John's intention? Obviously, by showing to John that his belief concerning his neighbor is mistaken and

---

[81]Skinner, *B. F. D.*, p. 147.
[82]*Ibid.*, p. 149.

false. It would be absurd to suggest that, as Skinner does, that one goes after something called "John's intention" which has to be caught and changed. I readily grant that this example is simple and that there are many complex situations and behaviors which call for detailed analyses. But this admission on my part in no way implies that Skinner and his behavioral scientists possess some recondite principles not already known to the layman. Thus it is perfectly in order to dismiss Skinner's jargon of contingencies and reinforcement as pedantic, pretentious, and trivial.

I now consider Skinner's treatment of the difficulties arising in the design of a culture. He writes:

> The applications of a science of behavior to the design of a culture is an ambitious proposal, often thought to be utopian in the perjorative sense, and some reasons for skepticism deserve comment. It is often asserted, for example, that there are fundamental differences between the real world and the laboratory in which behavior is analyzed. Where the laboratory setting is contrived, the real world is natural; where the setting is simple, the world is complex; where processes observed in the laboratory reveal order, behavior elsewhere is characteristicslly confused. These are real differences, but they may not remain so as a science of behavior advances, and they are often not to be taken seriously even now.[83]

Further, comparing behavioral scientists (as designers and controllers of culture) with physicists, Skinner observed:

> ... Fortunately for them [physicists], much of what is now known in their field came to be known as the result of research and its technological uses, and did not need to be considered until formulations were well advanced. The behavioral scientist has had no such luck. He is all too aware of his own behavior as part of his subject matter. Subtle perceptions, tricks or memory, the vagaries of dreams, the apparently intuitive solutions of problems—these and many other things about human behavior insistently demand attention. It is much more difficult to find a starting point and to arrive at formulations which do not seem to be simple.... The interpretation of the complex world of human affairs in terms of an experimental analysis is no doubt often oversimplified.... A science of behavior is not

---

[83]Skinner, *B. F. D.,* p. 158.

yet ready to solve all our problems, but it is a science in progress, and its ultimate adequacy cannot now be judged.[84]

All this is true and is indeed a candid recognition of the enormity of the difficulties confronting the designer of culture. But besides expressing unbridled optimism and pointing out that traditional practices too were unsuccessful in the design of culture, Skinner says nothing as to how he would go about changing and controlling the behavior of people on a mass-scale by the methods of operant conditioning. It seems that it is far easier to talk endlessly about such grandiose programs than to implement them. Nowhere does Skinner throw even a dim light on the actual mechanics of modifying and controlling the behavior of people on a large scale, not just in some specific aspects but with respect to all aspects—social, political, economic, religious, ethical, scientific, artistic, aesthetic, sexual, etc. I should confess my inability even to conceive of how Skinner would go about accomplishing his goal in a programmatic manner with respect to a society as a whole. In saying this I do not mean to imply, however, that it is *logically impossible* to accomplish; all I am drawing attention to is that the implementation of the program is so difficult as to make it reasonable to doubt its feasibility. And Skinner's talk about "planned diversification"[85] is irrelevant to the question of implementing his design in the first place. Unfortunately, optimistic rhetoric, no matter how persuasive to the faithful, is not an answer to this all important question. The disappointing conclusion, then, is that Skinner's program is no more than the latest addition to that long list of utopian dreams and delusions which Skinner himself so jubilantly discredits.[86]

Another serious obstacle confronting the designer of culture, says Skinner, comes from the opposition to a new cultural design: "I wouldn't like it," or in translation [in the lingo of Skinner's scientific analysis], "The culture would be aversive and would not reinforce me in the manner to which I am ac-

---

[84]Skinner, *B. F. D.*, pp. 159-160.

[85]*Ibid.*, p. 162.

[86]*Ibid.*, p. 184-185 (his remarks on the failure of Robert Owen's utopian experiment at New Harmony).

customed."[87] Emphasizing that this difficulty deserves careful consideration, Skinner suggests how to overcome it:

> ... The problem is to design a world which will be liked not by people as they are now but by those who live in it. "I wouldn't like it" is the complaint of the individualist who puts forward his own susceptibilities to reinforcement as established values. A world that would be liked by contemporary people would perpetuate status quo. It would be liked because people have been taught to like it, and for reasons which do not always bear scrutiny. A *better* world will be liked by those who live in it because it has been designed with an eye to what is, or can be, most reinforcing.[88]

Skinner scarcely disguises here his self-assigned role of the seer and the messiah. For he claims to know what would be liked by people who are not yet here. How does he know? We are not told, however. The truth of the matter is quite the reverse: It is not as though Skinner is designing a culture on the basis of a knowledge of what people who will live in it would like or dislike; rather, he designs a culture with an eye to what he thinks (*feels?*) they ought to like and then reinforce them to like it. In order to successfully answer this charge, Skinner should tell us *how he knows* what reinforces those people most. Skinner cannot avoid playing one or the other of the two roles besides that of the empirical scientist: the seer, if he claims to know what reinforces unborn generations of people; the reformer, if he claims he would give them what he thinks is good for them. Out of modesty, I suppose, he chooses the latter. He should be commended for not concealing this choice; for he explicitly says:

> The word reform is in bad order, for it is usually associated with the destruction of reinforcers—"the Puritans have cut down the maypoles and the hobby horse is forgot"— *but the design of a new culture is necessarily a kind of re-form,* and it almost necessarily means a change of reinforcers."[89]

But since he claims to reform culture, not according to his own feelings, but on the basis of a knowledge of what people in the

---

[87]Skinner, *B. F. D.,* p. 163.
[88]*Ibid.,* p. 164.
[89]*Ibid.,* p. 163 (emphasis added).

future like and dislike, he is inevitably a seer too. Thus Skinner is a man for all seasons, a seer, a moralist, a *re-former,* and an empirical scientist. And it is only natural that he chose to carry the burden of all these roles, for after all, according to him, survival is the *only* value according to which a culture is eventually to be judged. Under the guiding hand of such "scientific wisdom," who can dare doubt the survival of his culture? We are told that man's abolition has been long overdue.[90] Now that it will be finally accomplished, man no longer prevails and endures but basks in the glory of his sheer survival.

Granting that a complete break with one's past is impossible and that the designer of a new culture is himself culture-bound, Skinner says that therefore "to some extent he will necessarily design a world *he* likes."[91] It is difficult not to detect a Biblical ring about this utterance, for God, too, we are told, after creating the world and beholding it was immensely pleased with it. Be that as it may, the problem here is: What gives the designer the right to design a culture *he* likes and impose it upon others? Perhaps, the designer is a kind of God; or, at least, he should think of himself as one, for otherwise how can he know what is good for the yet unborn and accordingly provide them with it? It is also noteworthy that the pronouncement "The ultimate sources [of what people call 'goods'] are to be found in the evolution of the species and the evolution of the culture"[92] is dubious and unenlightening. First, it gives the misleading impression that there are some ultimate sources; and second, it is difficult to see how and precisely in what sense the evolution of the species and the culture could be the ultimate sources of what people call 'goods,' for, in light of the claim that *survival is the only value,* it follows that anything that insures survival is good, not what people call 'goods.' This objection can only be refuted by showing that the two, namely, things people call 'goods' and things that ensure the survival of a culture analytically imply each other. I cannot see how Skinner can show this.

90Skinner, *B. F. D.* p. 200.
91*Ibid.,* p. 164.
92*Ibid.,* p. 164.

Skinner now prepares himself to face that menacing bull—the problem of determinism-versus-freedom. If someone is looking for the paradigm of an exercise in question-dodging and ambiguity, here is one:

> It is sometimes said that the scientific design of a culture is impossible because man will simply not accept the fact that he can be controlled. Even if it could be proved that human behavior is fully determined, said Dostoevsky, a man "would still do something out of sheer perversity—he would create destruction and chaos—just to gain his point. . . . And if all this could in turn be analyzed and prevented by predicting that it would occur, then man would deliberately go mad to prove his point." The implication is that he would then be out of control, as if madness were a special kind of freedom or as if the behavior of a psychotic could not be predicted or controlled.[93]

Dostoevsky, for all we know, may be talking about psychotics but that is not his point. It is rather that the prediction that a certain man will behave in a certain way under certain circumstances can be falsified by him. Put differently, the problem here is a reflexive problem, in that the prediction itself becomes one of the factors determining the man's behavior. Thus if X predicts that Y will go to a midnight underground movie tomorrow and if Y has knowledge of this prediction, Dostoevsky's point is that it is possible for Y to falsify this prediction by, say, staying home or taking a walk. Dostoevsky is not claiming that madness is a kind of freedom, although it is conceivable that sometimes the falsification of a prediction may take the form of violent and destructive acts. It depends upon several factors, for example, how strongly Y is committed to proving X's prediction false. Thus, in the above example, it is conceivable that Y, instead of going to a movie as predicted, may drive down to X's home, wake him up at midnight, and shoot his wife or child, thereby giving a resounding proof that he did not go to a movie, contrary to the prediction. We may, however, agree with Skinner that it is sheer madness for Y to have chosen this way of falsifying X's prediction. One may even call him a 'psychotic.' But none of these refutes Dostoevsky's

---

[93]Skinner, *B. F. D.*, pp. 164-165.

point that a man can falsify a prediction if the prediction is part of his knowledge. It should be made clear, however, that this is so has no bearing upon the metaphysical problem of determinism-versus-freedom. A metaphysical determinist may still argue that Y's behavior is determined by the event, namely, X's predicting. On the other hand, a metaphysical libertarian will argue that the determinist's argument is irrelevant insofar as Y has clearly shown that it is in his power to act contrary to the prediction. In short, the problem of determinism-versus-freedom is not an empirical-scientific problem but a metaphysical-dialectical problem. Nothing empirical can solve the problem one way or other. Ignoring all these considerations, Skinner charges Dostoevsky with having maintained that madness is a special kind of freedom and that the behavior of a psychotic could not be predicted or controlled. Before proceeding further, let me call attention to a few more points here. No one denied that the behavior of a psychotic can be predicted or controlled. But not every person who defies a prediction is a psychotic, not even everyone who defies a prediction in a violent manner. It would be absurd to define a 'psychotic' as one who defies a prediction. But such are the definitions one would be led to as a consequence of dogmatic adherence to one or the other side of what is essentially a metaphysical issue—in the present case, Skinner's thoroughgoing determinism, which is a metaphysical dogma and not an empirical-scientific position.

Nevertheless, Skinner says that "There is a sense in which Dostoevsky may be right."[94] But if he is willing to concede this much to Dostoevsky, why does Skinner attack Dostoevsky in the first place? As a matter of fact, this concession on Skinner's part is not an admission that his criticisms of Dostoevsky are unwarranted. On the contrary, it is only a means by which to assert a fantastic generalization about the mental health of writers and artists. Thus Skinner writes:

> . . . A literature of freedom may inspire a sufficiently fanatical opposition to controlling practices to generate a neurotic if not psychotic response. There are signs of emotional instability in those who have been deeply affected by the literature. We have no better indication of the plight of the traditional libertarian

---

[94]Skinner, *B. F. D.*, p. 165.

than the bitterness with which he discusses the possibility of a
science of technology of behavior and their use in the intentional design of a culture.[95]

One wonders what all this has to do with the issue of
determinism-versus-freedom. Having no arguments by which to
support his own metaphysical dogma of determinism, Skinner
attacks the authors of literature of freedom in general; he
attacks Dostoevsky in particular for being a major figure in the
production and propagation of such literature which, according
to Skinner, is dangerous and could only turn its readers into
neurotics if not psychotics. Skinner also does not hesitate to
unleash impersonal ad hominems and draw the shaky generalization of a causal connection between the literatures of freedom
and emotional instability. He bitterly laments the serious
obstacles posed by the literatures of freedom to the possibility
of an intentional design of culture. Having had his share of ad
hominems, Skinner immediately calls our attention to Arthur
Koestler's and Peter Gay's admittedly harsh and less than polite
comments on behavioristic psychology. But these are no worse
than Skinner's own remarks on his adversaries, in particular what
he calls "the philosophies and literatures of freedom." And
when he complains that "name-calling is common"[96] and docu-
ments that Koestler and Gay are both guilty of it, he forgets
that he has just indulged in some name-calling himself. How
explain this apparently paradoxical *behavior*? It is not hard to
explain it if we realize that name-calling results when one is
passionately committed to a thesis, equally passionately opposed
to its antithesis, and is unable to defend his own thesis and
refute the antithesis. This observation holds equally with respect
to Skinner and his opponents. Both are advancing metaphysical
theses, not empirically verifiable scientific theses. And no
amount of argumentation can settle the issue at hand, in the
present instance that of determinism-versus-freedom. Each party
can do no more than assert and reassert its thesis with ever
greater force of conviction; and finding that the opposing party
has not given up its counterthesis, the disputants move from

---

[95]Skinner, *B. F. D.,* p. 165 (emphasis added).
[96]*Ibid.,* p. 165.

intellectual argumentation to innuendo, from discussion to diatribe, and from neutral discourse to name-calling. The point, then, is that Skinner's attacks on the literatures of freedom do not constitute a refutation of the metaphysical thesis of human freedom, but are only a forceful and ferocious assertion of the equally undemonstrable counter-thesis of determinism. I agree with Skinner, however, that it is ridiculous to blame behaviorism for all our ills.[97]

Skinner now asks the crucial question: Who controls the controller? He writes:

> ... The designer of a culture comes under fire because explicit design implies control (if only the control exercised by the designer). The issue if often formulated by asking: Who is to control?[98]

As an answer, he says:

> The great problem is to arrange effective counter-control and hence to bring some important consequences to bear on the behavior of the controller.[99]

Also,

> Self-government often seems to solve the problem by identifying the controller with the controlled. The principle of making the controller a member of the group he controls should apply to the designer of a culture. A person who designs a piece of equipment for his own use presumably takes the interests of the user into account, and the person who designs a social environment in which he is to live will presumably do the same. He will select goods or values which are important to him and arrange the kind of contingencies to which he can adapt. In a democracy the controller is found among the controlled, although he behaves in different ways to the two roles.[100]

Let us leave aside for the moment the ethical aspects of intentional design and control of behavior and ask whether Skinner has in any way answered the question: Who controls the controller? He says that we should look not at the controller but at the contingencies under which he engages in control.

---

[97]Skinner, *B. F. D.*, p. 166.
[98]*Ibid.*, p. 168.
[99]*Ibid.*, p. 171
[100]*Ibid.*, p. 172.

What precisely does he mean by this? His analogy of the controller with the manufacturer is irrelevant and unilluminating. It is true that a manufacturer is guided by profit-making and hence must take into account the interests of potential users of his product. But what has this to do with the designer and controller of culture? In the case of the manufacturer there is the built-in controlling element which requires that he take into account the interests of the users of his product. Is there a parallel built-in controlling element in the case of the controller of society as a whole? In short, what is the reason to believe, as Skinner certainly seems to ask us to, that the controller takes into account the interests of those whom he intends to control? If the controller has enough power and if accumulation of more power for himself is his goal, why would he care about the interests of those he seeks to control? To revert to the analogy of the manufacturer, we know that some manufacturers produce goods detrimental to the well-being of their users and still manage, through various advertising techniques, to sell them well and make considerable profits. That is, the manufacturer is not necessarily guided by compassion and concern for his customers. His aim is to make profit and he often does by selling with impunity bad and harmful products. In a similar manner, there is no a priori reason to believe that the designer and controller of culture is concerned about the interests and welfare of the people he intends to control.

Skinner writes:

> ... The archetypal pattern of control for the good of the controllee is the benevolent dictator, but it is no explanation to say that he acts benevolently because he is benevolent or because he *feels* benevolent, and we naturally remain suspicious until we can point to contingencies which generate benevolent behavior. Feelings of benevolence or compassion may accompany that behavior, but they may also arise from irrelevant conditions. *They are therefore no guarantee that a controller will necessarily control well with respect to either himself or others because he feels compassionate.*[101]

This may very well be the case but *there is no guarantee either that a controller who necessarily controls well is con-*

---

[101] Skinner, *B. F. D.*, p. 170 (emphasis added).

*cerned about the interests and well-being of those whom he
plans to control.* Skinner is again doing shadowboxing with
feelings of benevolence and compassion. He has given no reasons
for us to believe that the controller of culture cares about the
interests of the controlled. Skinner's allusion to the Indian
mystic Ramakrishna is totally irrelevant in this context:

> . . . It is said that Ramakrishna, walking with a wealthy friend,
> was shocked by the poverty of some villagers. He exclaimed to
> this friend, "Give these people one piece of cloth, and one
> good meal each, and some oil for their heads." When his friend
> at first refused, Ramakrishna shed tears. "You wretch," he
> cried, ". . . I'm staying with these people. They have no one to
> care for them. I won't leave them." We note that Ramakrishna
> was concerned not with the spiritual condition of the villagers
> but with clothing, food, and protection against the sun. *But his
> feelings were not a by-product of effective action*; with all the
> power of his samadhi he had nothing to offer but com-
> passion.[102]

But is it necessary for feelings of compassion to be real and
authentic that they should be a by-product of effective action?
Further, whoever has claimed that compassion such as
Ramakrishna's is in itself sufficient to alleviate human misery?
What Skinner should show is that the man with the power to
control behavior and is capable of effective action to diminish
and eradicate human suffering and misery will necessarily use his
power to that end. It is not at all clear as to what Skinner
means when he says:

> . . . Although cultures are improved by people whose wisdom
> and compassion may supply clues to what they do or will do,
> the ultimate improvement comes from the environment which
> makes them wise and compassionate.[103]

Is this true? It will be true if an environment is so designed
that men living in it will tend to become wise and compassionate. But this is to beg the question, for what reason is there
to believe that the designer and controller of a culture will in
the first place design so. One begins to smell the dead mouse of
infinite regress—the designer and controller of a culture is

---

[102]Skinner, *B. F. D.*, pp. 170-171 (emphasis added).
[103]*Ibid.*, p. 171.

capable of compassion and wisdom because of his already being in an environment (designed by someone else) which made him so. And what made this prior designer design that kind of environment? and so on. I am neither suggesting that men cannot become compassionate and wise nor maintaining that they become so by some miracle. The question is: Are there any a priori reasons for which we should believe that those who have the power to design and control culture will do so with concern for the interests and well-being of their controllees? or that they will design a culture which will make men compassionate and wise? I submit that Skinner has not answered these questions besides merely asserting the irrelevant truism that ultimate improvement of the human condition can only come from effective action.

To say that "the designer of a culture is not an interloper or meddler. He does not step in to disturb a natural process, he is part of a natural process"[104] or that "there is a sense in which a culture controls itself"[105] is not an answer to the question: Who controls the controller? The first assertion is trivially true and irrelevant to the question; and the second is an espousal of a mystical faith in some innate power of culture to control itself or in some "natural morality in both biological and cultural evolution."[106]

Skinner's assertion that in a democracy the controller is found among the controlled[107] is no guarantee that democracies cannot be turned into tyrannical regimes by the designers and controllers of culture. Only someone who believes in the myth of the immutability of democracies can advance the argument that democracy provides effective counter-controls by which "to bring some important consequences to bear on the behavior of the controller."[108]

It should be clear by now that Skinner has no answer to the all important question: Who controls the controller? All he does is to ask us to have faith in the goodness, wisdom, and

---

[104]Skinner, *B. F. D.*, p. 180.
[105]*Ibid.*, p. 172.
[106]*Ibid.*, p. 173.
[107]*Ibid.*, p. 172.
[108]*Ibid.*, p. 171.

compassion of his designers and controllers. Skinner does not say this explicitly. It is, however, implicit in his purported answers, or rather in their futility, as has been shown in our analysis of them.

Emphasizing again the serious and menacing obstacles posed by the philosophies and literatures of freedom to the possibility of an intentional design and control of culture, Skinner writes:

> . . . Life, liberty, and the pursuit of happiness are basic rights. But they are rights of the individual and were listed as such at a time when the literatures of freedom and dignity were concerned with the aggrandizement of the individual. They have only a minor bearing on the survival of a culture.[109]

These observations lead us to ask again: Why is the survival of a culture the supreme value for the preservation of which freedom, dignity, and the individual should be subordinated and even sacrificed? We have seen that Skinner could not answer this question. All he gave us by way of an answer are rhetoric, dogmatic metaphysical assertions, tautologies, and impersonal ad hominems. Furthermore, what is to be done with those who believe the contrary—that a culture from which freedom, dignity, and the individual are banished is not only not worth surviving but should be opposed at all cost and prevented from coming to be? It is easy to imagine many who would say that they would rather see such a culture not survive and simply vanish away than live in it. But, then, Skinner's designers would say: Let us get to work before these people go crazy and psychotic.

To conclude, Skinner has failed to refute the thesis of human freedom. He merely told us that the idea of human freedom, particularly as presented in the philosophies and literatures of freedom, is a grave threat to the possibility of a science of behavior and to an intentional design and control of a culture. His answers to the important questions: Why should a man regard the survival of his culture as good? and who controls the controller? are no answers at all. For, as an answer to the first, he dogmatically asserts that survival is the *only* value according to which a culture is eventually to be judged, and that

---

[109]Skinner, *B. F. D.,* p. 180.

if a man's culture has not convinced him that there is good reason why he should be concerned with its survival so much the worse for his culture; and as an answer to the second, he simply exhorts people to have faith in the goodness, compassion, and wisdom of his designers and controllers of culture. These assertions are an integral part of Skinner's weltanschauung and have nothing to do with science. Weltanschauungs and philosophical perspectives are neither true nor false. One either accepts them or rejects them depending upon one's extra-scientific commitments, predilections, and preferences. But it is only fair that one be clearly told whether one is being given a weltanschauung or a weltanschuung disguised as science. For, after all, the humble still have the right to know whether the voice they hear is that of the scientist or of the prophet, moralist, and re-former.

# Chapter VI

## SKINNER'S VISION OF MAN

In this chapter, I shall discuss certain of Skinner's general views on man. It will be shown that they are essentially metaphysical theses and not scientific propositions open to check. It may be well to remind the reader that I have never maintained that there is anything objectionable against anyone having a metaphysic. What is objectionable, however, is to disguise metaphysics as science.

Discussing such concepts as 'aggression,' 'traits of character,' etc., Skinner says that the concept of contingencies explains the behaviors referred to by the former concepts. Thus he writes:

> ... The contingencies explain the behavior [called 'aggression'] quite apart from any state or feeling of aggression or any initiating act by autonomous man. ... The behavior they [traits of character] refer to can be explained in other ways. Some of it may be attributed to genetic idiosyncracies (and subject to change only through genetic measures), and the rest of environmental contingencies, which are much more important than is usually realized. Regardless of any normal genetic endowment, an organism will range between vigorous activity and complete quiescence depending upon the schedules on which it has been reinforced. The explanation shifts from a trait of character to an environmental history of reinforcement.[110]

As for cognitive activities, such as attention,

> ... We can arrange contingencies which ensure that an organism—even such a "simple" organism as a pigeon—will attend to one object and not to another, or to one property of an object, such as its color, and not to another, such as shape. The inner

---

[110]Skinner, *B. F. D.,* p. 186.

gatekeeper is replaced by the contingencies to which the organism has been exposed and which select the stimuli to which it reacts. . . . Our perception of the sun depends on what we do with respect to it.[111]

All this is true but only partly, for Skinner nowhere shows us how to define concepts such as 'aggression' and 'attention' wholly in terms of observable behavior and contingencies. We have shown in an earlier chapter that it is impossible to define them in such a manner. It is one thing to say that rough and incomplete behavioral translations of these concepts are fairly adequate for scientific work and quite another to claim, as Skinner does, that these can be given completely behavioral translations. Such extravagant claims as "the inner gatekeeper is replaced by the contingencies" and "it is the environment which acts upon the perceiving person, not the perceiving person who acts upon the environment"[112] are categorical claims asserting the total translatability of the above kind of concepts in exclusively behavioral terminology. The point of these remarks is that Skinner's claim that his science of behavior is wholly based on the observable is both unsubstantiated and false, insofar as concepts like 'attention' and 'aggression' are central to his science, as he himself seems to admit. It is important to note that I am not therefore suggesting that appeals be made to the autonomous man, in order to extricate ourselves from the difficulties of translating theoretical terms into behavioral terms. All I am saying is that a science claimed to be solely based on observational terms is a fiction. The upshot of these criticisms is that Skinner may be able to banish the autonomous man from his so-called science of behavior, but he can hardly banish theoretical terms. But if he resolves to banish them too, as he certainly claims to, "Skinner's doctrine (of radical behaviorism) may establish the technology of dog-training on a solid empirical basis but it will never reveal the inner mechanisms of a dog's handshake."[113]

---

[111]Skinner, *B. F. D.*, p. 187.

[112]*Ibid.*, p. 188.

[113]John P. Seward, "Choice-points in Behavior Research," *Scientific Psychology: Principles and Approaches,* ed. Benjamin Wolman, Basic Books, N.Y., 1965, p. 167.

I come now to an examination of the assertion that "the fact remains that it is the environment which acts upon the perceiving person, not the perceiving person who acts upon the environment."[114] Is this a fact? How is it known? How does Skinner prove this assertion? What sort of experiments are to be conducted in order to determine its truth? It seems to me that the organism and the environment are a continuum and it is only in abstraction that we separate the one from the other and say that the environment acts upon the organism and not the other way round. The organism and its environment are in constant interaction and it is therefore arbitrary and absurd to shift action exclusively to one or the other of the two. Thus when I am in an environment, the environment and I are simultaneiously present to each other, barring aside the times taken by lights, sounds, and other signals to travel back and forth. This is not to say, however, that the environment does not exist when I am not perceiving it. All that is meant here is that it is futile to try to trace the origin of action solely to the environment or the organism. Action and reaction are reciprocal, it being impossible for there to be one without the other. It is therefore nonsense to say that it is the environment which acts upon the perceiving person and not the perceiving person on the environment. Further, the terms 'action' and 'environment' are extremely ambiguous and unless they are clarified only equally ambiguous generalizations can be asserted. More importantly, the claim that it is always the environment that acts upon the organism is not potentially falsifiable (potential falsifiability is a distinguishing feature of scientific propositions), for an organism is always in some environment or other. Thus, it seems, all that Skinner is asserting is the innocuous truism that an organism is always in some environment or other. But from this truism it does not follow that it is the environment that acts upon the organism and not the organism upon the environment. The tilt toward the organism or environment, that is, the shifting of action to the organism or environment, is a general metaphysical bias, not a verifiable scientific thesis. How shaky such an assertion is can further be seen by considering the following observations:

---

[114]Skinner, *B. F. D.,* p. 188.

> ...A sudden or strong stimulus may break through and 'attract' attention, but the person himself seems otherwise in control. An analysis of the environmental circumstances reverses the relation. The kinds of stimuli which break through by "attracting attention" do so *because they have been associated in the evolutionary history of the species or the personal history of the individual* with important—e.g., dangerous—things.[115]

But what do the terms "evolutionary history" and "the personal history of the individual" mean here? The elements constituting the evolutionary history of the species or the personal history of the individual, through which the sudden or strong breakthrough of a stimulus is accounted for, are not at the moment observed. It is precisely to avoid a similar difficulty with having to assert causal connections over temporal gaps, Hull was compelled to postulate the concept of "habit strength," which is a theoretical concept not capable of a wholly behavioral explication. Moreover, Freud, too, tried to account for the presently observed behavior through episodes and events in personal history? Why, then, was he taken to task and his methods branded as unscientific and mythological? Freud may be mistaken in his particular explanations but that does not mean that he was unaware of the significance of personal history to explaining present behavior; nor does it mean that it is behavioristic psychology which has discovered such significance. The very fact that Skinner has to resort to such nebulous phrases as "the evolutionary history of the species" and "personal history of the individual" goes to show the desperate struggle of a science of behavior that pretends to be solely based on the observed and observable.

Consider now the following:

> ...We saw that a baby perceives his mother's face and knows it. Our *evidence* is that the baby responds in one way to his mother's face and in other ways to other faces or other things. He makes distinction not through some mental act of perception but because of prior contingencies.[116]

---

[115]Skinner, *B. F. D.,* pp. 186-187 (emphasis added).
[116]*Ibid.,* p. 187 (emphasis added).

What is it an evidence for that the baby responds in one way to his mother's face and in other ways to other faces or other things? If it is an evidence for saying that "the baby perceives his mother's face and knows it," it is appropriate to ask: What is the difference between the evidence and what it is an evidence for? That is, a distinction must be pointed to in order that we may say X is evidence for Y. In the present case, Skinner should tell us the difference between "the baby responds in one way to his mother's face and in other ways to other faces or other things" and "the baby perceives his mother's face and knows it." If he is unable to tell the difference between the two, Skinner is merely saying that "X is evidence for X," which is tautologous and does not say anything at all. More importantly, Skinner cannot in principle point to such a distinction because his science of behavior a priori precludes it by identifying perceiving and knowing with the observed responses. No wonder, then, Skinner's alleged explanations can only be unilluminating tautologies.

I turn now to a consideration of Skinner's treatment of consciousness. He complains that behaviorism has been unjustly accused of ignoring consciousness (or awareness) as a proper study of psychology. Saying that "the charge is a serious one and should be taken seriously,"[117] he promises to show us that "behaviorists have been responsible for the most vigorous discussion of the nature and use of what is called consciousness."[118] But what has he to offer in defense of this claim?

> ...Man is said to differ from the other animals mainly because he is "aware of his own existence." He knows what he is doing; he knows that he has had a past and will have a future; he "reflects on his own nature;" he alone follows the classical injunction "Know thyself."[119]

But all these observations on man and consciousness, ironically enough, are old traditional stuff one can easily find in any dusty philosophy textbook. They are part and parcel of that repository of the common man's wisdom called "common sense."

117 Skinner, *B. F. D.,* p. 190.
118 *Ibid.,* p. 166.
119 *Ibid.,* p. 190.

One wants to know what in particular are the allegedly rigorous discussions of behaviorists and their contributions to the study of consciousness. It is worth noting in the first place that Skinner's claim on behalf of behaviorism is dubious, because it is not at all clear whether he is saying that behaviorists have made some unique contributions to the study of consciousness or behaviorists have been responsible for some vigorous discussions (by others) of consciousness by their ignoring it and by denouncing those who do study it. There is little evidence for the former as is clear from Skinner's failure to produce any besides promises and rhetoric. The latter is certainly true, for other schools of psychology, particularly those influenced by phenomenology, have, by undertaking a serious study of consciousness, been battling against the behavioristic dismissal of consciousness as irrelevant and as a positive hindrance to a scienfific study of behavior. To be sure, Skinner says: "Any analysis of human behavior which neglected these facts would be defective indeed."[120] But what evidence has Skinner produced in support of his claim that behaviorists not only did not neglect consciousness but made some contributions to its study? We shall return to this question a little later. Let us consider now some more remarks of Skinner in the present context. Skinner continues:

> ... And some analyses do. What is called "methodological behaviorism" limits itself to what can be publicly observed; mental processes may exist, but they are ruled out of scientific consideration by their nature. The "behavioralists" in political science and *many logical positivists in philosophy have followed a similar line.*[121]

It should be emphasized in the context of these observations that if Koestler's paraphrase of behaviorism is approximately seventy years out of date,[122] Skinner's conception of scientific method is at least thirty years out of date. Logical positivism is a dead doctrine and no physicist or philosopher of science today claims any allegiance to it. Even Bridgman, a distinguished advocate of operationalism and positivism, while declaring that a

---

[120]Skinner, *B. F. D.*, p. 190.
[121]*Ibid.*, p. 190.
[122]*Ibid.*, p. 166.

concept is synonymous with the corresponding set of operations, explicitly stated as follows:

> ...If the concept is physical, as of length, the operations are actual physical operations, namely, those by which length is measured; or *if the concept is mental, as of mathematical continuity, the operations are mental operations, namely, those by which we determine whether a given aggregate of magnitudes is continuous.*[123]

And even if it is true that many logical positivists were methodological behaviorists in Skinner's sense, logical positivism as a philosophical dogma has nothing to do with how science, for example, physics, is actually done. It is a wise advice from Einstein "Don't listen to what a physicist says but look at what he does." Fortunately, physicists did not pay much heed to the doctrine of logical positivism. They went their own way both in theoretical and experimental physics producing triumph after triumph in quantum and relativistic physics. No wonder, then, under the influence of methodological positivism, behavioristic psychology and the so-called sciences of sociology and political science could point to no achievements of theirs even remotely comparable to those of physics and biology. These so-called behavioral sciences still remain little more than banal common sense wrapped in the thick mist of forbidding jargons and not sciences with predictive and explanatory power. It is correct, then, to say that Skinner, contrary to his oft-repeated claim, is not treading the path of physics and biology but that of logical positivism, a self-proclaimed spokesman of science which has nothing to offer but a priori dogmatic metaphysics.

Let us, however, continue and see what Skinner and his science of behavior has to tell us about consciousness. Skinner says that although mental processes are by their *nature* ruled out of scientific consideration' "self-observation can be studied, and it must be included in any reasonably complete account of human behavior."[124] What is the nature of mental processes by which they are excluded from scientific consideration? We are

---

[123]P. W. Bridgman, *The Logic of Modern Physics* (originally published in 1927), Macmillan, 1961, N.Y., p. 5.

[124]Skinner, *B. F. D.,* p. 190.

not told, however. It follows by Skinner's own admission that, insofar as mental processes by their very nature are excluded from scientific consideration but nevertheless can be studied, mental processes *cannot* be studied scientifically. Also notice the ambiguity here—it is mental processes that are by their nature excluded from scientific consideration but self-observation can be studied. The main issue is thus fully skirted for we do not know whether Skinner considers the study of self-observation as a study of mental processes and consciousness. Nevertheless, he immediately adds that

> ... Rather than ignore consciousness, an experimental analysis of behavior has stressed certain crucial issues. The question is not whether a man can know himself but what he knows when he does so.[125]

What precisely are these crucial issues and what light behaviorism throws on them, we shall presently see. In order to avoid changes of unfairness being brought against me, I shall quote Skinner in full:

> The problem arises in part from the indisputable fact of privacy: a small part of the universe is enclosed within a human skin. It would be foolish to deny the existence of that private world, but it is also foolish to assert that because it is private it is of a different nature from the world outside. The difference is not in the stuff of which the private world is composed, but in its accessibility. There is an exclusive intimacy about a headache, or heartache, or a silent soliloquy. The intimacy is sometimes distressing, (one cannot shut one's eyes to a headache), but it need not be and it has seemed to support the doctrine that knowing is a kind of possession.
>
> The difficulty is that although privacy may bring the knower closer to what he knows, it interferes with the process through which he comes to know anything. ... There are, of course, *natural contingencies* under which we learn to respond to private stimuli, and they generate behavior of great precision; we could not jump or walk or turn a handspring if we were not being stimulated by parts of our own body. But very little awareness is associated with this kind of behavior and, in fact, we behave in these ways most of the time without being aware of the stimuli to which we are responding. We do not attribute awareness to other species which obviously use similar private

---

[125] Skinner, *B. F. D.,* pp. 190-191.

stimuli. To "know" private stimuli is more than to respond to them.[126]

As regards consciousness, Skinner writes thus:

> The verbal community specializes in self-descriptive con-
> tingencies. It asks such questions as: What did you do yester-
> day? What are you doing now? What will you do tomorrow?
> Why did you do that? Do you really want to do that? How do
> you feel about that? The answers help people to adjust to each
> other effectively. And it is because such questions are asked
> that a person responds to himself and his behavior in the
> special way called knowing or being aware. Without the help of
> a verbal community all behavior would be unconscious. Con-
> sciousness is a social product. It is not only *not* the special field
> of autonomous man, it is not within range of a solitary
> man.[127]

I ask the reader to ponder these observations and evaluate
my contention that none of them is unknown to common sense
and that people have known them since long before a supposed
science of behavior came along. Neither the statements on
privacy nor those on consciousness can properly be claimed to
be the findings of behaviorists. Philosophers in both East and
West have long ago made these observations, only they did not
employ such "scientifically impressive" terms as "natural contingencies" and "private stimuli." Thus even a cursory look into
the Buddhist treatises is enough to convince anyone that the
Buddhist philosophers long ago concluded that consciousness,
language, and society are closely related phenomena. It is to be
noted that Skinner could not refrain from throwing a punch at
the autonomous man here as if someone maintains that there is
a necessary connection between consciousness and belief in souls
and the autonomous man. I am sure it would be of interest to
Skinner to know that Buddhist philosophers explicitly reject any
suggestion of an enduring self or soul by analyzing the whole of
existence into the Skandhas (the anattā doctrine). Thus, according to the Saṁyutta-Nikāya, "The body, monks, is soulless. . . .
Feeling is soulless . . . perception is soulless . . . the aggregates are

---

126Skinner, *B. F. D.*, p. 191 (emphasis added).
127*Ibid.*, pp. 191-192.

soulless . . . consciousness is soulless. [128]    In the Milindapañha,
Nāgasena teaches thus:

> Your majesty, I am called Nāgasena; my fellow-priests,
> your majesty, address me as Nāgasena; but whether parents give
> me the name Nāgasena, or Sūrasena, or Vīrasena, or Sīhasena, it
> is nevertheless, your majesty, but a way of counting, a term, an
> appellation, a convenient designation, a mere name, this
> Nāgasena; for there is no ego here to be found. [129]

Also, the Visuddhi-magga declares as follows:

> Just as the word "chariot" is but a mode of expression for
> axle, wheels, chariot-body, hole, and other constituent mem-
> bers, placed in a certain relation to each other, but when we
> come to examine the members one by one, we discover that in
> the absolute sense there is no chariot; . . . in exactly the same
> way the words "living entity" and "ego" are but a mode of
> expression for the presence of the five attachment groups [from
> (matter), feeling, perception, impulses, and consciousness], but
> when we come to examine the elements of being one by one,
> we discover that in the absolute sense there is no living entity
> there to form a basis for such figments as "I am," or "I"; in
> other words, that in the absolute sense there is only name and
> form. [130]

Analyses similar to those of the Buddhists are to be found
in the writings of David Hume:

> There are some philosophers who imagine we are every
> moment intimately conscious of what we call our self. That we
> feel its existence and its continuance in existence; and are
> certain, beyond the evidence of a demonstration, both of its
> perfect identity and simplicity. . . . For my part, when I enter
> most intimately into what I call myself, I always stumble on
> some particular perception or other, of heat or cold, light or
> shade, love or hatred, pain or pleasure. I never can catch myself
> at any time without a perception, and never can observe
> anything but the perception. . . . I may venture to affirm of the
> rest of mankind, that they are nothing but a bundle or
> collection of different perceptions, which succeed each other

---

[128] "Saṁyutta-Nikāya," *A Source Book in Indian Philosophy*, ed. S. Radhakrishnan and Charles A. Moore, Princeton University Press, N.J., 1967, p. 280.

[129] "Milindapañha," *A Source Book in Indian Philosophy*, ed. S. Radhakrishnan
and Charles A. Moore, Princeton University Press, N.J., 1967, p. 281.

[130] "Visuddhi-magga," *A Source Book in Indian Philosophy*, ed. S. Radhakrishnan and Charles A. Moore, Princeton University Press, N.J., 1967, pp. 284-285.

with an inconceivable rapidity, and are in a perceptual flux and movement.[131]

Returning to self-observation, Skinner says:

> ... self-observation is only a preliminary to action. The extent to which a man *should* be aware of himself depends upon the importance of the self-observation for effective behavior. Self-knowledge is valuable only to the extent that it helps to meet the contingencies under which it has arisen.[132]

I cannot help remarking that these observations are neither new nor brought to light by the behaviorists.

Concerning complex cognitive activities such as thinking, discriminating, generalizing, and abstracting, Skinner writes:

> ... Rather than suppose that it is therefore autonomous man who discriminates, generalizes, forms concepts or abstracts, recalls or remembers, and associates, we can put matters in good order simply by noting that these terms do not refer to behavior.[133]

But again I should point out that none of this is new. In the West it is as old as Hume and in the East as old as Buddhism:

> There is not a person who is in possession of character, *thoughts* and deeds; but character, thoughts, and deeds themselves are the person. There is *no ego* in you ... *that thinks your thoughts* and shapes your character, but your thoughts are thinking, and your character itself is the nature of your very self.[134]

As regards self-control (or self-management) Skinner says:

> Self-control, or self-management, is a special kind of problem solving which, like self-knowledge, raises all the issues associated with privacy. ... It is always the environment which builds the behavior with which problems are solved, even when the problems are to be found in the private world inside the

---

[131]David Hume, *A Treatise of Human Nature,* ed. Selby Bigge, Clarendon Press, London, 1896, I, IV, VI, (252).

[132]Skinner, *B. F. D.,* p. 193.

[133]*Ibid.,* p. 193.

[134]Paul Carus, *Nirvana, A Story of Buddhist Psychology,* Open Court, Illinois, 1902, p. 38.

skin. *None of this has been investigated in a very productive way, but the inadequacy of our analysis is no reason to fall back on the miracle-working mind.*[135]

I leave it to the reader to judge for himself the profundity and scientific character of Skinner's observations on self-control and privacy. In any case, in view of his own admission that none of the cognitive phenomena have been investigated in a very productive way, it seems reasonable to conclude that Skinner's claim that behaviorists have been responsible for vigorous discussion of the nature and use of consciousness (or awareness) is false and unwarranted.

Let us examine now Skinner's views on physiological psychology. As has been pointed out in an earlier chapter, Skinner's science of behavior systematically leaves out of consideration the neurophysiological aspects of the organism. Neurophysiology is ruled out as irrelevant and unnecessary for a science of behavior insofar as the latter is claimed to be concerned with studying overt behavior and not what goes on under the skin. That is, as far as Skinner's science of behavior is concerned, the organism is empty. But Skinner now writes:

> In shifting control from autonomous man to the observable environment we do not leave an empty organism. A great deal goes on inside the skin, and physiology will eventually tell us more about it. It will explain why behavior is indeed related to the antecedent events of which it can be shown to be a function.[136]

These remarks give us the impression that Skinner believes that physiology has a significant role in a science of behavior. Such an impression is mistaken as is evident from the further remarks:

> ...Many physiologists regard themselves as looking for the "physiological correlates" of mental events. Physiological research is regarded as simply a more scientific version of introspection. But physiological techniques are not, of course, designed to detect or measure personalities, ideas, attitudes, feelings, impulses, thoughts, or purposes.[137]

---

[135]Skinner, *B. F. D.,* pp. 194-195.
[136]*Ibid.,* p. 195.
[137]*Ibid.,* p. 195.

I submit that this negative characterization of physiology is a gross distortion and totally unwarranted. It is hard to see why there should be any a priori objections to a study aimed at establishing the physiological correlates of the so-called mental events. Unless someone believes that ideas, thoughts, purposes, etc. mysteriously pop up, it makes sense to ask: What are the neurophysiological states and events correlated with such phenomenological states as feeling, thinking, desiring, intending, perceiving, laughing, weeping, etc.? Instead of being a hindrance to our understanding of behavior, neurophysiological correlations throw much light on the physico-chemical mechanisms in the organism and enhance our understanding of behavior as the interaction between the organism and the environment. The neurophysiological mechanisms will enable us to establish causal links from stimulus through the organism to the response, instead of leaving the observed S-R correlations, as behaviorism does, hanging up in the air.

> The basic theme of these investigations [physiological analyses of behavior], and therefore their promise for the future, has been the elucidation of the neurological mechanisms underlying the behavior. Through such study, motivated behavior can be related to physiological regulation; the internal environment and its endocrine, metabolic, chemical, and physical makeup can be related directly to the nervous system, and vice versa; and the many learned and unlearned factors that control motivated behavior can be uncovered and organized into a meaningful whole. *Out of these advances comes not only a basic scientific understanding, but the distinct possibility of practical application in the medical and social control of obeisity, sexual deviation, aggression, and other disorders of motivation as well as in the development and management of normal, healthy drives and motivations . . . there is great promise that the nature of reinforcement will be elucidated and related to neurological mechanisms in motivation. Through such investigations we should gain understanding of the keys that shape and control behavior.*[138]

Neurophysiological psychology thus enlarges the possibilities of behavior control in a manner totally out of reach of

---

[138]"The Biology of Behavior," *Biology and the Future of Man,* ed. Philip Handler, Oxford University Press, N.Y., 1970, pp, 399-402 (emphasis added).

Skinner's so-called science of behavior. Injection of chemicals and electrical probing and surgery of the brain have already proven more effective methods of modifying and controlling behavior than the tedious methods of operant conditioning (the methods of the kennel and the circus). Neurophysiological research has thrown considerable light on dreaming, memory, learning, etc. on which Skinner's science has little to say. Physiological psychology, unlike behaviorism, employs theoretical concepts and does not shy away from postulating hypothetical entities. This is not a defect; quite the contrary, through such devices it establishes systematic connections in the behavioral matrix made up of the organism and environment and hence explains and predicts behavior.

Ignoring all these considerations, Skinner derogatorily describes physiological psychology as simply a more scientific version of introspection. It is well-known that the term 'introspection' has been in bad odor and ill-repute for sometime now. By associating physiology with introspection, Skinner hopes to build a case of guilt by association. But such hopes are doomed to failure because they are not founded in fact. 'Introspection' is a term that refers to phenomenological states and acts, such as willing, desiring, and feeling, which supposedly are directly accessible to the subject and hence are not open to public observation. But this has no bearing on neurophysiological inquiry, for physiological states and events studied by the physiologist are publicly observable. That there are correlations between the phenomenological-introspective states and neurophysiological states does not mean that the physiologist *observes* introspection. The language of introspection and that of physiology are each appropriate to a different level of description. That there are correlations between the two levels does not mean that we have to deny one level in order to affirm the other; nor does it mean that statements in one language are fully translatable into statements of the other. Thus Skinner's rhetorical question: "How can a personality, idea, feeling, or purpose affect the instruments of the physiologist?"[139] is an absurd and nonsensical question. What affect the instruments of

---

[139]Skinner, *B. F. D.,* p. 195 (emphasis added).

the physiologists are not these but their physiological correlates.

It is amazing, then, that Skinner puts physiological psychology on the same level with introspection. Whereas introspection provides no scientifically useful information about what goes on under the skin, neurophysiology certainly does. It is therefore fallacious to say that "... Since they are *both directed inward* they have the same effect of diverting attention from the external environment."[140] The phrase "they are both directed inward" is worth noting for its strikingly misleading character. True, introspection is directed inward and nothing scientifically useful can come out of it. But neurophysiology is directed inward only *metaphorically,* for its object of study, namely, neurophysiological states and events, are publicly observable, just as the environment in which the organism is situated and its overt behavior. It is also to be noted that in charging physiology with diverting our attention away from the external environment, Skinner is reiterating his dogma that external environment is the sole determinant of behavior and hence that the physiology of the organism is irrelevant and unnecessary for constructing a science of behavior. We have, however, already drawn attention to the shortcomings of such a science of behavior and there is no need to repeat them here. In view of his remarks on neurophysiology, Skinner's statement that "in shifting control from the autonomous man to the observable environment, *we do not leave an empty organism*"[141] is merely a concession for courtesy, since he at the same time tells us that neurophysiology as the study of what goes on inside the organism can only serve to divert our attention from the all-important external environment.[142] Before leaving this point, it is important to further document Skinner's negative evaluations of the significance of neurophysiology to a science of behavior. Thus, commenting on the study of psychology in the Soviet Union, Skinner observes:

> ... The psychology being taught, even in education, is couched in neurological terms, and everyone makes this very clear. A teacher's college director will tell you that he is concerned with the higher nervous activities. *At the moment, Russians cannot*

---

140Skinner, *B. F. D.,* p. 195.

141 *Ibid.,* p. 195.

142 *Ibid.,* p. 195.

*have an objective science of behavior such as we have in this country,* because it would be considered idealistic.[143]

It is interesting that while he looks upon his own science as objective Skinner regards the neurophysiological psychology of the Russians as non-objective. I suppose it does not take much conditioning to work oneself into such an unquestionably objective frame of mind.

Before closing this chapter, I shall examine Skinner's theses concerning individualism and self-control. He writes:

> One of the great problems of individualism, seldom recognized as such, is death—this inescapable fate of the individual, the final assault on freedom and dignity. . . . Some religions have made death more important by picturing a future existence in heaven or hell, but the individualist has a special reason to fear death, engineered not by a religion but by the literatures of freedom and dignity. It is the prospect of personal annihilation. The individualist can find no solace in reflecting upon any contribution which will survive him. He has refused to act for the good of others and is therefore not reinforced by the fact that others whom he has helped will outlive him. He has refused to be concerned for the survival of his culture and is not reinforced by the fact that the culture will long survive him. In the defense of his own freedom and dignity he has denied the contributions of the past and must therefore relinquish all claim upon the future.[144]

There does not seem to be any basis for these observations concerning the individualist. There is nothing about an individualist as such which would enable one to a priori assert that he is not concerned with the survival of his culture, that he refuses to work for the good of others, and that he is immune to reinforcement by the fact that those whom he helps will outlive him. It is patently false to say that, for example, Locke, Rosseau, Jefferson, Lincoln, or Gandhi, who are certainly known to be great individualist, were not concerned with the survival of their cultures or refused to work for the good of others. How could it be maintained that these men, in defense of their own freedom and dignity, had denied the contributions of the past

---

[143]*B. F. Skinner: The Man and His Ideas,* E. P. Dutton & Co., Inc., N.Y., 1968, pp. 97-98 (emphasis added).

[144]Skinner, *B. F. D.,* p. 210.

and must therefore relinquish any claim upon the future? In order to answer these criticisms and objections, Skinner would have to say that he does not mean any of these men by the term 'individualist.' But, then, to whom does the term properly apply? It is not immediately clear to me. In any case, it seems reasonable to assume that according to Skinner an individualist is one who produces literatures of freedom and dignity or is deeply affected by them. But such a characterization fits very well the persons mentioned above. And it would be false to say that these men were not concerned with the survival of their cultures and refused to work for the good of others. It should be clear by now that Skinner means something different by the term 'individualist': one who resists control by others. Even so, it does not follow that one who resists control by others (presumably under the influence of the literatures of freedom and dignity) is necessarily not concerned with the survival of his culture and refuses to work for the good of others. Skinner's remarks on the individualist are thus both unwarranted and unsubstantiated. He is led to such an unsupported and blatantly false conclusion by mixing up two different points: 1. fear of death and personal annihilation and 2. concern for survival of one's culture and doing good to others.

It is absurd to maintain that someone who is not afraid of death is necessarily concerned with the survival of his culture and works for the good of others. How, then, was Skinner led to such strange and unmistakably false observations and assertions? It is not hard to answer this question—Skinner attributes all evils to the autonomous man and thinks that the autonomous man is the source of lack of concern for the survival of one's culture as well as of one's refusal to work for the good of others. In his unmitigated zeal to discredit and dethrone the autonomous man, Skinner fails to see that there is no logical connection between belief in the autonomous man and lack of concern for the survival of culture and refusal to work for the good of others.

It is possible, however, that Skinner wants to say that the individualist is so concerned and preoccupied with his own freedom, dignity, and death that he tends to be extremely selfish and consequently lacks concern for the survival of his culture and for the good of others. This may be so. But it is a much larger claim that fear of death and belief in freedom and dignity invariably result in lack of concern for one's culture and for the good of others.

Skinner's message is clear. He regards as evil men who resist control by others. Who are the others? The self-appointed guardians of culture, namely, Skinner's behavioral scientists (the intentional designers and controllers of culture). If so, Skinner should frankly say that he is defining a new concept of individualist as one who resists control by Skinner and his designers and controllers of culture rather than try to derive that concept in a tortuous and futile manner from "fear of death."

This brings us to Skinner on self-control and culture controlling itself:

> A scientific analysis of behavior dispossesses autonomous man and turns the control he has been said to exert over to the environment. The individual may then seem particularly vulnerable. He is henceforth to be controlled by the world around him and in large part by other men. [145]

But does this not mean, then, that the individual is simply a victim? Skinner answers as follows:

> ...Certainly men have been victims, as they have been victimizers, but the word is too strong. It implies despoilation, which is by no means an essential consequence of interpersonal control. But even under benevolent control is the individual not at best a spectator who may watch what happens but is helpless to do anything about it? Is he not "at a dead end in his long struggle to control his destiny?" [146]

Further,

> It is only autonomous man who has reached a dead end. Man himself may be controlled by his environment, which is almost wholly of his own making. The physical environment of most people is largely man-made. . . . The social environment is obviously man-made—it generates the language a person speaks, the customs he follows, and the behavior he exhibits with respect to the ethical, religious, governmental, economic, educational, psychotherapeutic institutions which control him. The

---

[145]Skinner, *B. F. D.*, p. 205.
[146]*Ibid.*, p. 205.

evolution of a culture is in fact a gigantic exercise in self-control.[147]

It is important to point out that these assertions are based on a subtle equivocation, for in the question: Is man not simply a victim? 'man' refers to individual man, whereas in "the evolution of a culture is a gigantic exercise in self-control" evolution and self-control are spoken of with respect to the human species. It may very well be the case that evolution is an exercise in self-control. But a man, such as C. S. Lewis, who cries 'victim' when he says ". . . the power of man to make himself what he pleases . . . means . . . the power of some men to make other men what they please,"[148] is talking about individual men but not about the abstraction called 'human species.' In reply to such cries, Skinner admits that it is inevitable in the nature of cultural evolution that some men control other men.[149] If so, Lewis is asking, what right some men have to control other men? Skinner attempts to answer this question by resorting to the notion of two selves, the controller and the controllee, under the same skin. He writes:

> . . . The controlling *self* must be distinguished from the controlled self, even when they are both inside the same skin, and when control is exercised through the design of an external environment, the selves are, with minor exceptions, distinct. The person who unintentionally or intentionally introduces a new cultural practice is only one among possibly billions who will be affected by it. If this does not seem like an act of self-control, it is only because we have misunderstood the nature of self-control in the individual.[150]

It is obvious that Skinner and the 'victim-crier' are using the term 'self-control' in different senses and hence there is certainly a serious misunderstanding. And to give a stone to a man asking for bread is indeed a gross misunderstanding. C. S. Lewis need not deny that an individual X may intentionally introduce a cultural practice in order that he (Lewis) may ask: why some other person Y should be controlled by X via the

---

147Skinner, *B. F. D.*, pp. 205-206.
148Quoted by Skinner in *B. F. D.*, p. 206.
149Skinner, *B. F. D.*, p. 206 (emphasis added).
150*Ibid.*, p. 206.

cultural practice. His point is rather that to say both that some men like X control persons like Y and that Y still has self-control is absurd. To repeat, Lewis' point is quite straight-forward: What right has X to control Y? And having controlled Y, what sense does it make to say that Y still has self-control? Having himself admitted that it is inevitable that some men control other men, Skinner could not answer Lewis and hence resorts to the dubious notion of two selves under the same skin and to argument of inevitability from the pseudo-mystical concept of the nature of cultural evolution. In plain terms, his argument is: Whatever is a fact is also good and right. As a matter of fact, some men control other men. Therefore it is good and right that some men control other men.

Further, is everyone an innovator of cultural practices? Does every innovator of cultural practices have the power to impose those practices on others and thereby control their behavior? Is everyone both controller and controllee? As a matter of fact, only some men are both and hence have self-control. Even if it is inevitable in the nature of cultural evolution that some men control others, it does not make it consistent to say that X controls Y and Y has self-control. But since Skinner holds that it is inevitable in the nature of cultural evolution that some men control other men, it is only ap-propriate that he should see intentional design and control of culture in harmony with the very nature of cultural evolution.

# *Chapter VII*

## CONCLUSION

The following are the conclusions of the present study:

1. Skinner's so-called science, by restricting itself to overt behavior, can only describe and control limited sectors of behavior at the molar level. Insofar as it categorically rejects theoretical concepts, it lacks explanatory and predictive power. By refusing to take into account the physiological structure and constitution of the organism, it can throw no light on why a given stimulus draws a certain response from a certain organism. For this reason, its methods for manipulating the behavior of organisms are limited to classical and operant conditioning techniques. Consequently, Skinner's science of behavior cannot explain why and how operant conditioning is possible in the first place. Further, these methods are tedious, time-consuming, and are unsuitable for behavior modification and control on a large scale, such as required in the intentional design and control of a culture as a whole. In sharp contrast, behavioral biology and neurophysiological psychology are not only capable of providing a scientific understanding of behavior and thereby explaining and predicting it but also have great promise and potential for effectively modifying and controlling behavior on a large scale.

2. Skinner's claim that in constructing a science of behavior he is following the path of physics and biology is simply false. For physics and, to a lesser extent, biology are as much theoretical as experimental and freely make use of theoretical concepts and postulate hypothetical entities which enable one to construct extraordinarily complex theories which are put to test via their observable consequences. It is therefore false and

misleading to say that progress in these sciences has been achieved by ignoring and neglecting hypothetical entities and mediating states and turning attention to the exclusively observable.

3. Contrary to his claim to follow the methodology of physics and biology, Skinner, on his own admission, is following logical positivism, which is not a science but an outdated, short-sighted, and sterile philosophy of science. And like all doctrinnaire philosophies, it is an a priori dogmatic metaphysics.

4. Skinner's attempts to translate value judgments into wholly behavioral vocabulary are a dismal failure. His purported translations are unilluminating tautologies. His attacks on Karl Popper's thesis that it is impossible to derive normative statements from factual statements completely miss Popper's point— Popper is concerned with the *logical* problem of deriving norms from facts, not with the futile ontological problem of the existence of the autonomous man. Popper's thesis is compatible with both the affirmation and denial of the autonomous man.

5. Skinner's claim to have expelled the autonomous man and thereby demonstrated the thesis that all behavior is determined by external environment and hence that man does not have freedom is an empty claim. For the problem of determinism-versus-freedom is not an empirical-scientific problem. It is a metaphysical-dialectical problem to which everyone has his own solution depending upon his Weltanschauung.

6. Skinner has thoroughly failed to answer his own question: Why should a man regard the survival of his culture as good? His answer that the question does not really need an answer at all and that if a man's culture has not convinced him that there is good reason why he should be concerned with its survival so much the worse for his culture is not an answer but a flat and bald proclamation of his own values and biases.

7. Almost all of his attacks on people who use mentalistic terms in describing persons and their behavior are highly contrived and unsupported. Without taking the trouble to find out what these people mean by these terms, he attributes to them belief in the existence of some mysterious and intangible entities supposedly denoted by such terms.

8. Whenever he is hard pressed for an explanation, Skinner

invokes such pseudo-mystical notions as nature of cultural evolution, vague and ambiguous concepts as genetic endowment, and the blanket explanatory concept of contingencies, much as his opponents appeal to the autonomous man.

9. Skinner's observations concerning consciousness, privacy, and knowledge as well as the so-called cognitive activities such as thinking and discriminating, are little more than common sense and can easily be found in any elementary philosophy text.

10. Skinner could not produce any evidence to his claim that behaviorists have been responsible for vigorous discussions of the nature and use of consciousness. The truth of the matter is that behaviorists a priori rule out consciousness from scientific consideration and vehemently denounce those who do study it as being unscientific, metaphysical, or simply tender-minded.

11. It is ture, however, that the behaviorists' exclusion of consciousness as a subject worthy of their scientific study was responsible for vigorous discussion of the subject by others.

12. Skinner's arguments from the concept of fear of death to the conclusion that an individualist can neither be concerned with the survival of his culture nor work for the good of others are an unparalleled exercise in distorted logic. It is not surprising that his arguments also lead to the equally absurd conclusion that one who is concerned with the survival of his culture and works for the good of others is necessarily neither an individualist nor afraid of death.

13. While he untiringly expounds his grand program for the design and control of culture through his science of behavior, Skinner does not even hint as to how he would implement that program on a mass-scale.

14. Skinner has no answer to the all important question as to who controls the controller except exhorting us to have faith in the inevitability of democracy. By proposing the notion of two selves, namely, the controller and the controllee, under the same skin, he thinks that somehow by making the controller also the controllee, democracy "can bring some important consequences to bear on the behavior of the controller."[151]

15. Skinner has no arguments as to why we should believe

---

[151]Skinner, *B. F. D.,* pp. 171-172.

that his designers and controllers of culture will work for the good of those whom they intend to control. He merely asks us to have faith in their goodness, compassion, and wisdom.

16. Skinner holds that survival is the supreme value for the realization of which men should sacrifice their misguided, false, and dangerous notions of freedom, dignity, and the individual. But to those who would say that a culture from which freedom, dignity, and the individual are banished is not worth surviving he has no reply other than the assertion that such people were not induced by their culture to work for its survival.

17. His description of physiological psychology as a more scientific version of introspection and as directed inward is at best a caricature and at worst egregious nonsense.

18. Most people's fear of Skinner's scientific utopia is unwarranted, because the methods of his science are pedestrian, crude, impracticable, and wholly inadequate for the task of designing and controlling a culture as a whole. More importantly, Skinner himself admits that these methods do not work as long as the controllees are not deprived of their power for critical reflection.[152] If anything, it is behavioral biology with its techniques of behavior modification and control that is to be feared, because it is an established fact that through these techniques man's physiological equipment can be drastically altered so as to turn him into a zombie. But behavioral biologists, unlike Skinner, are quietly conducting their researches and do not yet seem to have a prophet and re-former.

I wish to emphasize that I have never even remotely implied that Skinner's behaviorism is unimportant and useless. Quite the contrary, the work of Skinner and his followers is adequate for the modification and control of behavior in a limited sphere, although it certainly lacks explanatory and predictive power; more importantly, it serves as the phenomenological basis on which to construct a genuine science of behavior which can only arise out of the recognition that behavior is a function of both the organism and environment.

It seems appropriate to close this essay with the following lines:

---

[152]B. F. Skinner, *Walden II,* Macmillan, N.Y., 1946.

As Merleau-Ponty has said, psychological theories can account for everything except the psychology of their creators. Psychological theorists have been inclined to play God, to see things sub specie aeternitatis, egocentrically forgetting that as human beings they can only have a partial and fragmentary and situation-bound command of all the essential phenomena, but also forgetting how their own behavior transcends their own theoretical formulations.[153]

---

[153]Joseph Church, *Language and the Discovery of Reality*, Vintage Books, N.Y., 1966, pp. 211-212.

# BIBLIOGRAPHY

Achinstein, Peter, "The Problem of Theoretical Terms," *American Philosophical Quarterly,* II, No. 3, July, 1965.

Ayer, A. J., *Language, Truth, and Logic,* Dover Publications, Inc., New York, 1946.

————, ed., *Logical Positivism,* Free Press, New York, 1966.

Bridgman, P. W., *The Logic of Modern Physics,* Macmillan, New York, 1927.

Brodbeck, M., ed., *Readings in the Philosophy of the Social Sciences,* Macmillan, New York, 1968.

Brody, Baruch A., *Readings in the Philosophy of Science,* Prentiss-Hall, New Jersey, 1970.

Carus, Paul, *Nirvana, A Story of Buddhist Psychology,* Open Court, Illinois, 1902.

Chomsky, Noam, "The Case Against B. F. Skinner," *The New York Review of Books,* December 30, 1971, pp. 18-24.

————, *Problems of Knowledge and Freedom,* Pantheon, New York, 1971.

————, "A Review of B. F. Skinner's *Verbal Behavior,*" *Language,* 35 No. 1, 1959, pp. 26-58.

Church, Joseph, *Language and the Discovery of Reality,* Vintage Books, New York, 1966.

Delgado, Jose M. R., *Physical Control of the Mind,* Harper & Row, New York, 1969.

Eccles, J. C., *The Neurophysiological Basis of the Mind,* Oxford University Press, New York, 1953.

Feigl, H. and M. Scriven, ed., "The Foundation of Science and the Concepts of Psychology and Psychoanalysis," *Minnesota Studies in the Philosophy of Science,* Vol. I, University of Minnesota Press, Minneapolis, 1956.

Feigl, H., M. Scriven, and G. Maxwell, ed., "Concepts, Theories, and the Mind-Body Problem," *Minnesota Studies in the Philosophy of Science,* Vol. II, University of Minnesota Press, Minneapolis, 1958.

Feigl, H. and G. Maxwell, ed., "Scientific Explanation, Space, and Time," *Minnesota Studies in the Philosophy of Science,* Vol. III, University of Minnesota Press, Minneapolis, 1962.

Feyerabend, Paul K., "Explanation, Reduction, and Empiricism," *Minnesota Studies in the Philosophy of Science,* Vol. III, University of Minnesota Press, Minneapolis, 1967.

————, "How to be a Good Empiricist—A Plea for Tolerance in Matters of Epistemology," *Philosophy of Science, The Delaware Seminar,* Vol. 2, ed., B. Baumrin, Interscience Publishers, New York, 1963.

Fodor, Jerry A., *Psychological Explanation,* Random House, New York, 1968.

Govinda, Lama Anagarika, *The Psychological Attitude of Early Buddhist Philosophy,* Rider & Company, London, 1969.

Guenther, H. V., *Philosophy and Psychology in the Abhidharma,* Buddha Vihara, Lucknow, India, 1957.

Handler, Phillip, ed., "The Biology of Behavior," in *Biology and the Future of Man,* Oxford University Press, New York, 1970.

Hempel, Carl G., "The Theoreticians Dilemma: A Study in the Logic of Theory Construction," *Aspects of Scientific Explanation,* The Free Press, New York, 1965.

Hook, Sidney, ed., *The Dimension of Mind,* New York University Press, New York, 1960.

————, ed., *Psychoanalysis, Scientific Method, and Philosophy,* New York University Press, New York, 1959.

————, ed., *Language and Philosophy,* New York University Press, New York, 1969.

Hull, C. L., *Essentials of Behavior,* Appleton-Century, New York, 1943.

————, *A Behavior System,* Yale University Press, New Haven, 1952.

Hume, David, *A Treatise of Human Nature,* ed., Selby Bigge, Clarendon Press, London, 1896, I, IV, VI, (252).

Johanson, Arnold A., "A Proof of Hume's Separation Thesis Based on a Formal System for Descriptive and Normative Statements," to be published in *Theory and Decision.*

Körner, Stephen, *Conceptual Thinking,* Dover Publications, Inc., New York, 1959.

Krober, Alfred L. and Clyde Kluckhohn, "Culture: A Critical Review of Concepts and Definitions," published in the *Harvard University Peabody Museum of American Archaeology and Ethnology Papers,* Cambridge, 1952, Vol. 47, No. 1.

London, Perry, *Behavior Control,* Harper and Row, New York, 1971.

Margenau, Henry, *The Nature of Physical Reality,* McGraw-Hill, New York, 1950.

Martin, Michael, "Neurophysiological Reduction and Psychological Explanation," *Philosophy of the Social Sciences,* I, 1971, pp. 161-170.

Maxwell, Grover, "The Ontological Status of Theoretical Entities," *Minnesota Studies in the Philosophy of Science,* Vol. III, ed., H. Feigl and G. Maxwell, University of Minnesota Press, Minneapolis, 1962.

Monad, Jacques, *Chance and Necessity,* Alfred Knopf, New York, 1971.

Moore, G. E., *Principia Ethica,* Cambridge University Press, 1903.

Nagel, Ernest, *The Structure of Science,* Harcourt, Brace and World, Inc., New York, 1961.

Petrie, Hugh G., "A Dogma of Operationalism in the Social Sciences," *Philosophy of the Social Sciences,* I, 1971.

Popper, K. R., *The Open Society and Its Enemies,* Routledge and Kegan Paul, London, 1947.

————, *The Logic of Scientific Discovery,* Basic Books, New York, 1959.

Popper, K. R., *Conjectures and Refutations,* Basic Books, New York, 1962.

Puligandla, R., "Psychoanalysis, Behaviorism, and Psychotherapy," *Journal of Thought,* Vol. II, No. 3, July 1967, pp. 6-16.

Puligandla, R. and K. Puhakka, "Körner's Theory of Scientific and Metaphysical Directives," *The Journal of the Indian Academy of Philosophy,* Calcutta, 1970.

Quine, W. V. O., "Two Dogmas of Empricism," *From a Logical Point of View,* Harper and Row, New York, 1963.

————, *Ontological Relativity and Other Essays,* Columbia University Press, New York, 1969.

Radhakrishnan, S. and Charles A. Moore, ed., "Samyutta-Nikaya," *A Source Book in Indian Philosophy,* Princeton University Press, New Jersey, 1967.

—————, "Milindapanha," *A Source Book in Indian Philosophy*, Princeton University Press, New Jersey, 1967.

—————, "Visuddhi-magga," *A Source Book in Indian Philosophy*, Princeton University Press, New Jersey, 1967.

Russell, Bertrand, *Human Society in Ethics and Politics*, Mentor Books, New York, 1962.

—————, *Human Knowledge: Its Scope and Limits*, Simon and Schuster, New York, 1948.

Scheffler, Israel, *The Anatomy of Inquiry*, Alfred Knopf, New York, 1963.

Scriven, M., "A Study of Radical Behaviorism," *Minnesota Studies in the Philosophy of Science*, Vol. I, University of Minnesota Press, Minneapolis, 1956, pp. 89-130.

Seward, John P., "Choice-points in Behavior Research," *Scientific Psychology: Principles and Approaches*, ed., Benjamin Wolman, Basic Books, New York, 1965.

Skinner, B. F., *Beyond Freedom and Dignity*, Alfred Knopf, Inc., New York, 1971.

—————, *The Man and His Ideas*, E. P. Dutton and Co., Inc., New York, 1968.

—————, *Walden II*, Macmillan, New York, 1946.

—————, *Science and Human Behavior*, Macmillan, New York, 1953.

Stevenson, C. L., *Ethics and Language*, Yale University Press, New Haven, 1960.

Toulmin, Stephen S., *Foresight and Understanding*, Harper and Row, New York, 1963.

Turner, Merle B., *Philosophy and the Science of Behavior*, Appleton-Century-Crofts, New York, 1967.

Wann, T. W., ed., *Behaviorism and Phenomenology*, The University of Chicago Press, Chicago, 1964.

Wilson, J. T., ed., *Current Trends in Psychology and the Behavioral Sciences*, Pittsburgh University Press, Pittsburgh, Pennsylvania, 1954.

Wisdom, J. E., "Science Versus the Scientific Revolution," *Philosophy of the Social Sciences*, Vol. I, 1971.

Wolman, Benjamin, *Contemporary Theories and Systems of Psychology*, Harper and Row, New York, 1960.

—————, ed., *Scientific Psychology*, Basic Books, New York, 1965.

Wooldridge, Dean E., *The Machinery of the Brain*, McGraw-Hill, New York, 1963.

—————, *Mechanical Man*, McGraw-Hill, New York, 1966.